The Mentor Ship

Imagined, initiated, compiled, produced, edited
and partially written by.....

Tim Paulsen

and

Ken Young

ISBN-13: 978-0968349533

Dedication

This book is dedicated to our mentors and to our readers, who we hope will be inspired by the stories held within these pages. May the experiences and concepts here help you grow in your own journey as a mentor to the next generation. Our mentors have provided us with a wealth of experience and knowledge. They have unlocked their individual vaults containing a wealth of years of experience; they have reached deeply inside to train us and inspire us to higher levels of accomplishment. They have taken the time to show us the way, by exposing us to their successes and failures. The lessons we have learned from them have been powerfully beneficial and profound. These lessons have enabled us in many instances to expand our influences in our own firms, by making better-informed decisions that often result in greater success.

A thank you is also sent out to our bosses over the years who have recognized the value of continuing education, which has provided the tools to help us to learn, grow and become better equipped to be more effective. Training and development is an important complement to mentoring.

To function at our highest levels, the dual forces of continued training and dedicated mentors are invaluable for propelling us forward. Hop on board the "Mentor Ship", there is a cabin reserved for you. Be a mentor, you'll be glad you did!

...Ken Young

Introduction

It may have been a mistake. It could have been a tactical maneuver in a battle to burn some ships that got out of hand; it might be blamed on careless smoking or a Centurion with a lengthy list of seriously overdue books and a unique method to clear his record. The cause is still in dispute, but not the result.

Some two thousand years ago, some of Caesar's legions were responsible for the single greatest loss of an archive of knowledge, the burning of the library in Alexandria.

There is nothing new about progressing in our profession or any other. People get older, we expect wiser too as they learn from successes and mistakes and then shuffle off into retirement. But the speed and numbers are rather dramatic these days with the boomers (born between 1946 and 1964) moving along, there are 10,000 people EVERY DAY hitting retirement age. That does not take into effect downsizing and 'off sizing (moving off shore) and capsizing that often affect those of who may be the most seasoned and experienced, but also most expensive to their firm.

Tim Paulsen & Ken Young

Forget somebody walking out the door with a stapler or a box of pens. They are walking out with years of experience, hard won most of it, and when it's gone... it's gone. They say if you do not learn from your mistakes, you are condemned to repeat them. True enough – but it is a lot cheaper and much less expensive not to mention the scrapped knees and torn and tattered egos to learn from the mistakes and the success of others.

Many of us come from societies that do not pay the right amount of attention to our elders. It is called the 'road less traveled' for a reason. Once Lewis & Clarke found the North West Passage, people didn't rush out and say 'that's nice for them' and try to find their own way – they learned from the success and mistakes of those who went before them.

Lucky for us that they have not yet left the building or they aren't so far removed that we can't still hear them, enjoy some stories and learn along with them.

The stories are short, sometimes funny and always engaging. The stories are theirs but I take full blame for the title of the credit & collection life lesson.

...Tim Paulsen

Contributing Mentors

Special thanks to men and women of the credit profession who truly believe in "paying it forward":

Alana White

Andry Sichka

Andy Steele

Barry Aronoff

Bill Lindala

Bob Simon

Carole Stevens

Christine Fisher

Cliff Mearns

David Holloway

Declan Flood

Geoffrey Last

Gregg Gregory

Kathleen Palmer

Ken Young

Len Sklar

Lily Soliman

Lorne Booth

Martin Sher

Mark Silverthorn

Michelle Davy

Pam Krank

Paul Dover

Peter Kotzer

Phyllis Miller Saavedra

Ray Casola

Robert C. Karau

Robert Lorenzo

Stephen Coyle

Stevan Gan

Tim Paulsen

Tracey Skipp

TABLE OF CONTENTS

The Mentor Ship

"Time to Wake Up"[1]

By: Robert C. Karau

A Dwarf Standing on Shoulders

In my 35+ years of working in the credit and collections field, I have had a number of opportunities to mentor others and also to be mentored. I received mentorship training through my CFDD (Credit and Financial Development Division of NACM) chapter and experience joy and personal growth through mentoring others.

As a manager for 28 of those years, I have learned that an effective manager must also play the role of mentor with employees. Many times, this type of mentoring happens organically in effective managers and leaders. I have often seen results of this organic mentoring in my personal work experience

---

[1] "The tough life may force you awakened"...Toba Beta, *My Ancestor Was an Ancient Astronaut.*

when people who I trained and mentored were recommended and assumed four of the five management positions I previously held.

Effective mentorship goes beyond training and knowledge. Mentorship is a process that helps an individual discover their strengths, develop their talents and awaken their potential. Knowledge is a tool but how you use that tool distinguishes the maestro from the student. Training alone focuses on the present while development focuses on the future.

In my mentorship training, I learned that "mentor" comes from The Odyssey. Odysseus had asked his friend, Mentor, to help watch over his son Telemachus while Odysseus was away in the Trojan Wars. Twenty years later, the goddess of wisdom, Athena, disguised herself as Mentor to provide Telemachus with critical advice to investigate what happened to his father. This was definitely a time of growth and learning for Telemachus and as he learned more about his father, he learned more about himself. An awakening occurred.

Organic mentoring does not mean that you need to be a friend to everybody. A good mentor is a great encourager but must also help the mentee to also confront and recognize their weaknesses. I believe a mentor is someone who "lifts up" the mentee but this also means that they are more aware of both their strengths, individual potential and their weaknesses. As a leader and mentor, how we do this is also very important. Steve Jobs once remarked that "My job is not to be easy on people. My job is to take these great people we have and to push them and make them even better." As Diego de Estella observed: "A dwarf standing on the shoulders of a giant may see farther than the giant himself."

While training is fairly transactional in nature, development and mentoring can be transformational. In some ways, it involves awakening an individual's potential. In one instance, I received a call from a former employee's family requesting that I come and speak at Steve's funeral. It was interesting to me that even though I had dismissed Steve from his position and no longer worked with him, Steve had told his family that no one else he worked with had impacted his life and made him feel as valuable as I had. While I showed Steve his faults and pushed him to do better work, he still maintained his respect. He knew that I cared about him. At his exit interview, Steve told the head of personnel that he was sorry he let me down as I had given him what he needed to succeed and had shown him that he could do it if he tried. He said working with me had changed his life.

As credit and collection professionals, we work in an ever-changing and evolving workplace. Technology, artificial intelligence, automated process management and pre-programmed workflows are re-defining certain functions within our departments. As our workplace continues to change, employees need to grow beyond simple technical proficiency. We need employees who can adapt and thrive in a very fluid environment. I believe that the need for mentorship in our age is critical to people's abilities to adapt to change. Author Alvin Toffler said: "The illiterate of the 21st century will not be those who cannot read and write, but those who cannot learn, unlearn, and relearn." As mentors, we need to develop people and make sure they are not only able to learn and perform their current jobs but that they can perform at high levels in tomorrow's workplace. Robert Frost once said that "we must not just view ourselves as teachers but also awakeners." That is a mentor to me. This type of mentorship can transform our businesses and the lives of those we reach.

Robert C. Karau

Bob is Manager of Client Financial Services for Robins Kaplan LLP, a large national law firm. He has worked in the credit and financial services profession for over 35 years.

Bob has been a credit manager for the Valspar Corporation, Principal Resources and Hoffer's Inc. In addition, Bob has done extensive consulting on Sarbanes Oxley, corporate governance and compliance for Grant Thornton LLP and is currently serving on an advisory team for a large national e-Billing software company that specializes in the legal industry.

Bob serves as an Area Director and board member for NACM's Credit and Financial Developmental Division (CFDD) and is a past president of his local CFDD He is currently a member of the NACM National Law Forum Credit Group and also serves as a Director on his local NACM affiliate board.

The Importance of Being Ernest

By Geoff Last CCP., CCE.

Tough Messages and Long Term Relations

I think the greatest successes I've had, have been the long term relationships I've built with customers and they seem to be the most rewarding. What stands out in particular is how some of them developed. The credit novice may come to the assumption that he always needs to be a sycophant, always striving to please each customer.

More often than not, we have a tough message to deliver for our employers, and it is not always easy to tell a customer that his or her account is on hold, or that you will have to take some sort of aggressive collection action, perhaps even realizing on our legal rights. You do no one a service when the message is not delivered in a clear, concise format that leaves no room for understanding.

Once, when I attended a retail establishment to collect on a past due account, I was paid by the owner/investor, but at threatening knifepoint. He wanted to make sure I understood that the payment was being proffered with the condition that all future orders would be processed with his approval only. I indicated my understanding of the arrangement and we became close friends until his passing.

In another instance, I attended a customer to advise the principal that I was proceeding with exercising my lien rights on a job he had just completed but had not paid for. After exercising these rights, he ultimately paid the account and we continue to dine together regularly, with our spouses.

Confrontation often leads to negotiation which can lead to resolution; the important factor is relationship building. In another instance, a debtor attended my place of business to protest my placing his account with an attorney. In no uncertain terms, he indicated that such action would cause him to go to our senior management to have my employment terminated. I nonetheless, stood my ground, but continued the dialogue. After much further discussion, and the conversation completed without resolution, he left, but not before wishing me good luck in my future employment. The account was paid a few days later.

Geoffrey Last CCP., CCE.

Geoffrey Last is the National Credit Manager at Rexel Canada. He had been Director of Credit for Anixter Canada Inc. for about 18 years and with Anixter for 18 years and with Canada Wire & Cable for 8 years prior.

He is a Fellow of the Credit Institute of Canada, a member of the National Credit & Financial Executives Forum, a Certified Credit Executive (NACM) and has attended NACM's Graduate School of Credit Management. He has chaired the Legislation Committee of the Credit Institute and is currently a Director of NACM Canada. He has lectured in the past on technology solutions for the credit profession.

Tim Paulsen & Ken Young

I Left My Part in San Francisco

By Len Sklar

Love Competition – Hate Competitors!

Many years ago, I owned and operated a collection agency in San Francisco. Naturally, due to the size of the metropolitan area, we had lots of competition, and, whenever we had a competitor, we almost always came out on top.

The 'why' and the 'how' had a lot to do in part with traditional selection followed by training and development. But, it was also due in part to how we instituted ways to reduce stress:

1.) We had a 6 foot high, heavy bottomed clown that collectors could smack, and it came back for more.
2.) Another stress reducer was some small voodoo dolls with pins that they could stick in them. These were very popular after a nasty phone call.

I was also alert to offer compliments and

appreciation on a regular basis for almost anything that was done well. In fact, surveys show that the single most effective motivational technique is just that - show appreciation on a steady basis. Too many managers are afraid to do that, possibly out of the fear that the employee may ask for a raise.

In my seminar business, I didn't have a non-competition agreement with my other seminar leaders - I had 11 of them - and two started their own seminar businesses, in competition with me. (I trained them well).

Len Sklar

...is the author of "The Check is NOT in the Mail". Prior to starting his own company in 1970, he spent 14 years with Proctor & Gamble, Dow Chemical and IBM. He has trained thousands of business people and is an authority on collection psychology and technique.

Customers Do Not Pay a Company!

By Barry Aronoff B., COMM., CCP.

Who's on First? You!

Decide early to be a jack of all trades. We are called upon to be the go to people: the experts, in tax issues, Terms and Conditions, maintenance procedures, the fireman to put out the fires, the guy or girl with all the answers.

1. Be a sales oriented credit manager. Show the sales department you care and respect them and in turn, they will support you when the need arises. (And, it will!)

2. Taking on the role of a psychologist is a necessary evil. Listen and you will learn a lot about your customers (sometimes more than their intent).

3. Credit Management is a great field, yet not for the weak at heart.

4. No glory/no thank you. Welcome to the club of credit managers. If you are in this to have everyone thank you and agree with you change professions- it is not for you. Thank yourself, pat yourself... 'cause *"that is it baby"*.

5. Right side up! Customers pay people not companies. Train yourself and then your team to get on the good (right) side of the customer.

6. Join groups, credit groups, discussion groups, read articles, take training courses. Remember there is always something to learn, even for old guys like me.

7. Hold your ground, and do not cave if you truly believe in your decision. If you are overridden, don't take it personally. It gets you off the hook. And that is not always a bad thing.

8. Get out! The day of credit managers sitting at their desk making a decision is over. You need to go out, visit your customer know who they are.

9. Do not hesitate to make a decision. Analyze, digest the facts, and yet do not

delay for fear. We all make mistakes even credit managers like me with 30 years of experience. Those who fear will never succeed. Remember through failure comes success.

10. Don't kick yourself too hard or too long! If you get hit with a bad debt, do a post mortem, and move on. Do not punish yourself, know that we have all been there. You cannot be afraid to take risk because of this. Good risk will win 9 out of 10 times.

Barry Aronoff... B., COMM., CCP.

Barry Aronoff has been a Credit Manager for over 30 years with varied roles as Collections Manager, Assistant Credit Manager, Financial Service Manager, and now Ontario Divisional Credit Manager at Rexel, Canada.

He holds a CCP with the Credit Institute of Canada, served as a mentor for graduates of the Credit Institute of Canada, has given training sessions on various topics of Credit Management to Sales, Staff, Management and the Ontario Electrical Association. He has also spent 13 years of his life dedicated to coaching organized baseball from House League right up

Tim Paulsen & Ken Young

to Triple AAA in Mississauga.

Half Baked Credit Sales

By Andy Steele, CCP., FICB.

A Credit Sale That Makes No Sense – Makes No Cents!

Once when I was on vacation a credit application came in from one of our sales personnel for a company in Quebec which was approved by our trade insurer for credit insurance. The application listed a bakery with an excellent record of paying their bills.

But what the credit analyst and trade insurer missed was the type of product and where it was being shipped to. It was not going to the company warehouse, but to a new location in the outskirts of Montreal.

When a second shipment was sent out, our transportation company driver noticed something funny and notified his dispatch who called me. The driver said that while trucks where being unloaded to a delivery dock, another truck was being loaded. Since all the employees where speaking Russian he could not understand what was going on. He was hesitant to drop off our load until he got clarification.

As soon as I looked at the credit application, I notice the sold to party was a bakery and the application was signed at a business office and not the bakery office. My first question to the sales person was, *'Why is a bakery buying electrical products?'*

He said they were starting up a distribution centre to sell our products. When asked what was their experience in this type of operation and he said he didn't know, I told him to drop by their office. When he called back he said the unit was empty, completely cleaned out.

Later investigation determined that this was an identity fraud. With over a million dollars in debt, the legitimate business filed for court protection. The RCMP who investigated the fraud told me that this was a group of Russian's who set up the sting and that one of the members had convinced the owner of the legitimate business to sign the credit applications to make it easier for her bakery to get better deals on the products she purchases.

Not once did she realize she was purchasing high dollar electrical parts.

We were lucky. Most of our sales were insured and our loss was under $12 thousand dollars. Another firm lost well over one million.

1. Make sure your sales people are trained to ensure that the product they are selling, matches the product lines of the prospective customer. They should also visit the delivery site to ensure everything is in order.

2. When reviewing the credit application, check all the addresses of the business. Do their product lines match the type of product you are selling?

3. Credit applications must be signed by an authorized person in the company.

4. If necessary do a check with the government to find out who the directors of the company are.

5. Have a good rapport with your trucking company who can notify you of any concerns on delivery.

Andy Steele CCP., FICB.

...has held senior credit management positions with Hewlett-Packard, Cott Beverages and Nexans, Canada. Over the years he has consulted and contributed to the Credit Institute of Canada.

Building a Reservoir of Trust

By Ken Young CCP., CCP. Emeritus.

There is More to the Story

Making a decision solely on financial disclosure is like looking at a Rembrandt with only a couple of primary colors on the canvas. There is much more to the decision than financial disclosure alone. Developing healthy, business relationships built on trust and mutual respect is an important aspect of credit management. I recall meeting with a customer in Chicago who had just created a start-up entity. The owner had been CFO with a firm that had gone out of business recently.

After dialoging with the customer for a while, he provided access to their opening balance sheet and spent a considerable length of time sharing their business plan. The value achieved in this meeting was the fact that we were the first major supplier to extend credit, which the customer never forgot.

Another significant aspect was the fact that we took the time to meet him personally and tour the facilities. A genuine and trusting business partnership was forever established. Visualization of the operation in so many lines of business adds a unique and invaluable dimension.

The credit line and terms that were initially established were adequate to get the firm purchasing their requirements of our product line from us. However these credit aspects (credit availability and terms) would still need to be reviewed in a matter of months, once a historical payment pattern and actual business results were established. This allowed us to keep a close watch on the company as it was progressing, keep the credit reins tight initially, and secure significant business volume in a geographical marketplace that we did not have high volumes from previously.

Over many years it was very pleasing to see the client grow to have a very significant presence in the geographical marketplace as well as the industry overall. We don't always bat 100% in credit granting, but it is rewarding when you can look back and see the impact that was made due in large part to trusting business relationships. These partnerships, once established, can produce very substantial volume growth, profitability and shareholder value for both parties.

There is a story told of Jerry Rice – one of the best wide receivers in the history of the NFL When he was asked why he attended Mississippi State University when a very well-known college (UCLA) had been recruiting him, his answer was they were the only college to come to his house and pay a personal visit. They showed in a personal way that they cared. It is the same with customers, as so many of them are proud of their business and appreciate the time suppliers take to come to their premises and meet them.

Face to face meetings offer significant and intangible interactions that go way beyond words. These meetings are more likely to result in agreement and collaboration.

Customer visits for some companies are a road

less travelled; however, depending on the volume, profitability and growth potential, it is a road that cannot be ignored if a complete picture of the risk elements versus reward is to be painted.

If customer visits are not possible, it is still very worthwhile to cultivate customer relationships – although they are not as effective as in a face to face setting – in order to more fully understand and to capture the upside of risk.

Mark Cuban once said, "The NBA (National Basketball Association) is never just a business. It's always business. It's always personal. All good businesses are personal. The best businesses are very personal."

Developing and maintaining customer relationships that are built on trust are of prime importance in significantly impacting your firm's revenue growth, profitability, and shareholder value in achieving corporate and personal success.

Ken Young, CCP., CCP. Emeritus.

Ken Young has been a credit management

professional for over twenty-five years and has global experience in a broad range of industries including the food (aquaculture & beverage), chemical, manufacture, and transportation sectors.

Most recently he was the Credit & Collection Manager at PepsiCo Beverages Canada.

Ken was a founding member and advisor of NACM Canada (National Association of Credit Management). He has served on numerous boards, including the Credit Institute of Canada, the National Credit & Financial Executives' Forum, the Raw Material Credit Group and the International Center for Professional Collectors.

He has been awarded the highly esteemed CCP Emeritus award from the Credit Institute of Canada for distinguished and meritorious service for the advancement of credit education and the credit profession.

Consulting projects and keynote speaking with ICPC (International Centre for Professional Collections) include Brunei and Jamaica. He can be contacted at young.ken@hotmail.com or www.trpaulsen.com/credit

Fifty Percent of a Successful Conference?

By Tim Paulsen

Being There (Body <u>and</u> Spirit)

Early in my career at a retail organization, I attended a conference in California. For a number of sessions, I decided to take in the sun by the pool rather than go to the break out meetings.

It was much more pleasant by the pool, especially for a Canadian visiting a warmer climate and I told myself I knew most of the material and would have been bored by the presentation. Whether the latter was true or not, I suspect I missed out on a lot of valuable information and I am certain I did not make the important connections – a primary reason to attend in the first place.

The comedian Woody Allen said that fifty percent of life is just showing up. The same applies to conferences and meetings. I'm reminded of the Captain of a Norwegian fishing vessel who was asked if he or any members of the crew brought along their spouses. She said, *"When we fish, we fish, and when we ....,"* you can fill in the blanks from there.

I was to learn my lesson too late, that when you're on vacation, you go to the pool and sit in the sun. When you attend a conference – you work.

Another snake would be 'sober comments' at meetings. I don't mean alcohol related, that's an entire other book for me. I've a quirky sense of humor (I've been told) and didn't hesitate to share it during a meeting. A bit more listening and fewer jokes would have served me better. I know that all of us are a package deal and you have to take the good with the bad, but we can still make some adjustments. I wished I had turned it down a few notches on more occasions.

During a separate visit to California, I was told, "Don't write a book about collections, write articles and sell 'em to as many organizations as you can, people as you can. Those articles become chapters and after you have enough of them, you've got a book."

The same speaker, Frank Hardesty, who was teaching a collection seminar sponsored by American Management Association, also said not to write expecting to make much money. They market for this type of book is too small. However, it does get you recognition and will get you on the speaking and consulting circuit.

Tim Paulsen...

...is author of 'Paid in Full', 'Tipping the Scales, and recently, 'Sex, Lies & Negotiation Techniques'.

As the founder and Managing Director of ICPC (International Centre for Professional Collections) he has consulted, trained and been a keynote speaker across Canada and the United States and more than twenty other countries. Mr. Paulsen is the creator of *'SAGE – The Excuse Terminator'* and *'The CollectABILITY Index®.'* He can be contacted at tim@trpaulsen.com or www.trpaulsen.com

A 500 lb. Gorilla Sleeps Wherever He Wants

By Kathleen Palmer C

But, It Doesn't Mean You Don't Collect The Rent!

We shipped some product to Quebec for a multinational. They claimed they were tax exempt and we allowed the exemption. After a tax audit informed us they were not exempt and we had to pay the tax, we invoiced the multinational for the approx $1,500 in tax.

It remained unpaid. I eventually got a contact from the A/P dept. for a person in procurement who could assist me. That person never returned my calls, but when we finally did connect they referred me to their assistant. Now we were even more substantially overdue. I reviewed the information with the assistant, including the reasons they are not tax exempt, they understood, but had to verify the PO, product, and get the managers approval to pay the invoice.

Many follow ups, later, the assistant continued to have one reason after the other, why the invoice was not yet paid, but reassured me it would be paid once they presented all the information to the manager, who would approve the invoice for payment. And no, they did not need me to speak with the manager, they would handle it. Many more days continued to pass with going back and forth numerous times.

There were many reasons why this small amount travelled so far past due, not a huge amount (especially for our company), the customer was not a financial threat to us, payment of all other items were current, and I had faith in the fact that someone was speaking with me and was encouraged they agreed the invoice should be paid. However, I decided it was time to take another tactic.

I went to the web site of the multinational and looked up the name and contact info of their in house counsel. I prepared an email starting with "WITHOUT PREJUDICE" described my issue in detail; I attached all my communication, copy of the invoice, and requested immediate payment. I never did hear from the in house counsel, but the week after I sent my email to the in house counsel, I did hear from the assistant who confirmed the invoice was approved for payment and we should see a cheque the following week. And we did.

Moral of the story, I trusted what seemed to be a helpful person, as they were telling me all the things I wanted to hear, but in actual fact they were not doing anything to get the invoice approved for payment. So once I changed the dynamics of the scenario, it put that person in a position of having to deal with the issue. In collections we need to take alternative actions in many instances in order to obtain recovery of funds owed.

Kathleen Palmer CCP.

Kathy Palmer, CCP. manages the Canadian portfolio for Nexeo Solutions Canada Corp. She has been with Nexeo Solutions for the past 11 years and previously held credit management positions with Para Paints, Toshiba Canada and Signode Canada. Kathy is a member of the Credit Institute of Canada, the National Credit & Financial Executives Forum and the Raw Material Credit Group. She also previously

Tim Paulsen & Ken Young

chaired this group. Kathy continues to grow, mentor and be mentored while networking with fellow credit colleagues.

Join a Gang!

By Martin Sher

It takes a Community

"Individual commitment to a group effort – that is what makes a team work, a company work, a society work, a civilization work." – Vince Lombardi

Back in about 1995, I set up a benchmark group with a colleague of mine. We were both very active in ACA International and had become good friends.

Our idea was to recruit 6 or 7 people we liked, respected, and knew were successful in the collection industry. We thought it best, at first, to find people in different parts of the country. It did not matter what type of accounts each member collected, or if they were going to be a direct competitor or not. Integrity and confidentiality were a must if we were to share sensitive information with each other.

We shared financial statements twice a year, and had open and frank discussions about anything and everything about our businesses, families, and life situations. We helped each other recruit key employees, and shared documents and management compensation plans. We acted as a support group for each other when a life situation came up in anyone's life. We hosted a meeting at each one of our offices until we knew each other's operations and personnel intimately.

In time, the group grew to 18 people but with people selling or retiring, we are sitting at about 12 now. I think if you asked each of us *'what was the most important and valuable thing you did in your career for your business and yourself'*, I think it would be unanimous that it was this Vision Benchmark group.

We also have an active email discussion all year long to help us with the 'issue of the day'. It is nice to have a group of successful colleagues that you can call in and get an answer and some experience to any business problem.

I would imagine this idea would work in any

industry, for any group of like professionals.

Martin Sher

Martin is the co-CEO of AmSher Receivables Management, based in Birmingham, Alabama. He is the author of a number of books, including *"How to Collect Debts & Still Keep Your Customer!"* Martin also has a blog with great title, *"Skinny and Debt Free"*.

Stand Your Ground – Even if Sitting Down

By Paul Dover CCP.

Leverage, it helps

Credit is a funny business, but it is an essential aspect to any company's operation. You have to know and utilize the 4 C's, (capacity, capital, conditions and character) for sure, in your role as Credit Manager, but many other skills and attributes need to be put into play in order to be successful.

I had a classic example of this when I was in the electrical industry, where one of our customers, an electrical contractor, owed us just over $75,000 that had gone quite past due (over 90 days). Most of my collection efforts proved fruitless, so I did some homework.

This was the construction industry, which is governed by the Construction Lien Act of Ontario; it is a law that polices the flow of funds on any construction project, from the owner down through the hired General

Contractor, sub-trades and suppliers. This project was the addition to a Toronto High School - I contacted the architect (who was the payment certifier), and learned that payment was made 2 months ago to the General Contractor (who had hired my electrical contractor). I then contacted the General Contractor's accounts payable, and found out that my contractor was paid two days after the General had received their draw.

Thus armed, I had to revert to more drastic measures, so (with the approval from my boss), I put the account on hold. This generated action pretty quickly – it turns out that Nick (the owner & president of the company) was on a job not far from our company, and the next day, he came storming into my office (accompanied by a rather sheepish counterman, who said "Paul, he insisted on seeing the Credit Manager!"). The conversation went as follows:

Nick – "Are you the credit manager?"

Paul – "Yes I am."

Nick – "I hear that you've cut me off! How dare you! I've got a company to run, and projects to finish! I want to speak to your superior!"

Paul – "Well, Nick, let's look at the situation here: we've granted XYZ Electric just over $185,000 credit in materials for your operations, of which 40% is unpaid and past due over 90 days. And further, calls to your Accounts Payable and Controller have gone unanswered."

Nick – "Don't worry! You'll be paid shortly."

Paul – "Really Nick? And when will that be?? I also found out that you were paid your draw for this work over 2 months ago. You've spent our money!"

(At this point, all the fire went out of him, and he almost cowered back his response)

Nick – "Well, I had some immediate expenses I had to take care of."

Paul – "Well sir, if I'm not paid by the end of this week (this was Tuesday), I'm putting a lien on the project, which, as you know, will block any further draws to you until I remove the lien."

I was paid the overdue balance the next day,

plus the money due that month – his cheque was sent courier.

In that industry, very often the contractors were immigrant Europeans, just like Nick, who had worked hard, and built their companies into very successful operations – but they came from the old school, and often used intimidation in an attempt to rectify a situation. Nick was about 6 ft. tall, quite fiery, and my assistant told me afterward that she was quite amused to see this large Greek towering over me with his loud voice, and me, looking up at him with my responses.

But know your stuff – don't back down; they have no recourse...and 9 times out of 10, you'll not only get paid, but gain the respect of your customer.

Paul Dover CCP.

Paul Dover is Credit Manager at Polytarp Products, who make plastic bags and sheet film for the construction, food, packaging, agricultural and automotive industries. Paul has been a credit professional for over 30 years, he is the Past President, Toronto Chapter of the Credit Institute of Canada. He has given presentations on the Construction Lien Act to Construction Industry Credit Groups with Equifax Canada, together with Max Shafir, QC, a well-respected construction lawyer in the industry. He currently sits on the Board, Toronto Chapter of the Credit Institute of Canada, as Chairman, By-Laws Committee.

They Can Beat You Up, But Can They Catch You?

By Gregg Gregory, CCP.

How Fast a Runner are You?

One of my first jobs in credit was working for a Heavy Equipment distributor as a credit representative. Along with selling heavy equipment they were also in parts and service, and servicing the equipment they sold.

We had a customer in the far north who at the time was a very small parts customer. This customer is what I call a PITA account (Pain in the A..) as they required a lot of time and effort to collect with minimal results and usually we did not get paid until we had something he needed that no other supplier could provide.

One day I received a call from our Branch Manager in Sudbury who told me that this customer had one of their excavators in our shop for service, and that it was urgently required as the customer was about to start on a major project. I had always kept him advised of the issues with this customer so he would always contact me when this customer needed something. (The importance of building relationships with all customers both internal and external!!)

I called the customer, Bill, and much to my surprise he actually came on the line. At the time of my call the account was pushing 120 days and I had been calling for weeks trying to collect and he continually put me off with numerous excuses. I started my call by asking him how things were going for him and when could we expect payment of the past due balance. Bill made his usual excuses and ended by telling me that he had nothing for me at this time. At that point I started to discuss the new project with him. He got all excited talking about it telling me where it was, the size of the job and everything else. I then brought up that we were doing some service work on the excavator we had in our shop and he said yes he really needed to get it in tip top shape as he badly needed this machine to start the project.

That was when I dropped the bombshell on him. Bill, I'm really glad to hear about this project, but we still have a past due balance that needs to get paid. He again started with the excuses. Then I told Bill, unfortunately that machine will not be leaving the shop until we get a cheque for the past due. There was silence for about ten seconds and then he unloaded on me. You SOB (and other expletives deleted) I need that machine and I need it now and if you don't release that machine I will come down there and beat the Sh.. out of you!!!

I waited for a few seconds and then calmly and asked Bill how big he is? Bill replied that he was six foot four and 250 lbs. I then answered and said to him, Bill let me tell you, I'm 6 foot 2 and I weigh about 170 lbs and I can run like stink so good luck trying to catch me. Bill was silent again for about ten seconds and then he started to laugh and said alright you SOB, I will bring the cheque with me when I pick up the excavator.

The lesson I learned from this is not to outwardly react to what a customer may say to you. They may be angry or stressed out or may even be trying to get you off topic. By not reacting or buying into their emotion you can usually help to deflate or settle down the situation. Understanding their issues is the key to effective collecting and in building relationships. Trying to deflect these issues and using humour will stand you in better stead going forward.

About a month later, I was making a trip up north to see another customer and I decided to take a chance and go in to see Bill at his office. He looked at me with a mean look and came over to me. Before he got to me he started laughing and shook my hand and said, *'Good for you, you got me good'*, and yes he was six foot four and 250 lbs. Bill never did become a model account but from that day on we did have an understanding about paying his account, so whenever he needed something and he was past due he would call me to tell me he was bringing in a cheque.

Gregg Gregory, CCP.

Gregg Gregory, CCP has worked in Credit for over 30 years in various industries including, Lumber Products, Metals Distribution, Fine Paper Distribution, Construction, HVAC and Mechanical Distribution and has been a consultant in the Financial Services industry working in the Retail Sector. Gregg is a Fellow of the Credit Institute of Canada and has served as a Director on the Toronto Chapter, National Credit and Financial Executives Forum and on the executive of the Credit Institute of Canada.

'Ahem…Do I Now Have Your Attention?'

By Pam Krank

It's about Facts and Figures

I make my living as a credit manager for about 50 companies…working for all of them at the same time actually. Sometimes, it's difficult just to remember who I am and what company I'm representing at the moment, but there are always those clients' customers you just never forget.

Our job is to manage trade receivables for mid-sized manufacturers mostly with sales ranging from $100 million to $3 billion. Their customers are a varied bunch – from small contractors and professional service companies to large multi-nationals and government entities. Our job is to manage the trade receivables portfolio to maximize cash flow from the asset and sales opportunities.

Anyone who manages trade receivables knows that collecting receivables is easier than the process of managing the risk and credit exposures. We always know the slow-pay customers before they become past due, because we're assessing the risk of default and slow pay before the customer places their first order. Our job is to predict risk of bad debt as well as the risk of slow pay. Our client determines through their credit policy whether to take on the risks; we're just administrators of the policy.

Several years ago I was operating as a credit manager for one of our clients, a larger mid-market food manufacturer in the Midwest. They had a strategic customer in Florida who represented about five percent of their business. This client had a history that was troublesome on paper: past bankruptcy, ongoing lawsuits, owner convicted of past fraud activity, lots of slow payment history and existing past dues. When I inherited the $250,000 exposure (which was 85 percent past due) and performed the due diligence, my first thought was to reduce that balance....quickly! I wanted to eliminate that delinquency to keep my client from suffering a big loss.

My first encounter with this strategic customer was shortly after we started working for our client when we put the customer on hold for past dues as they weren't returning our phone calls or emails. Our client had never stopped any orders from shipping to this customer for past due reasons before we took over the management of the asset; that's one of the reasons the balance had grown too large. They just continued to ship as long as the customer was making some type of payments. Well, I needed leverage to reduce the past dues and without their cooperating by returning our calls, I figured I'd start by stopping the flow of orders to get the negotiating rolling.

Needless to say, when the owner of my client's strategic customer got wind of the hold situation, he called to chew me out for holding up shipments for his largest client, the biggest beverage company in the world. Unfortunately for the customer, I had already left the office that day to pick up my baby from daycare so he wasn't able to catch me in the office; one of my supervisors got an earful instead. The customer, not satisfied but determined, noticed my cell phone number on the email I had sent about the hold and called me just as I was wrapping up my baby daughter in her snowsuit at daycare. I will never forget this conversation.

Recognizing the Florida number, I handed my bundled baby to the daycare person and slipped into another room to take the call. It was a good thing I had my baby far from the phone when I answered so that her newborn ears didn't hear the swear words that customer was yelling to me. *"How DARE you put my g***!&!&n account on hold! What in the h*!*! do you know about servicing my account? Who in the f***%!! authorized you to withhold my orders and create a potential loss of my biggest customer?"* The cursing went on for about five minutes. Once he finished and there was no more to be said, I calmly advised him of my concerns about the risks with his business, explaining what I could remember from my notes (pre smart-phone days). Realizing my concerns were all valid and not refutable, the customer went silent for a moment before he calmly said, *"What will it take you to release my railcar?"*

I let him know that we needed a plan. I wanted to know that he would work with me to pay down the past dues and keep his account current with us. I needed him to allow his banker and CFO to discuss his cash situation with me and to understand the expected resolution/risk of the lawsuits so that I could get comfortable enough to offer a continued line of credit. After his angry, four-letter tirade, he calmed down and responded "okay; I understand". With the good faith understanding, I released his orders with a payment promise.

Two weeks later, I was on my way to visit him in Florida to see for myself what was happening. He showed me his books and his bank statement. He invited his banker to lunch with us, showed me the paperwork on the lawsuits, and explained the prior fraud conviction and subsequent bankruptcy. Spending time in his office, I was able to see this man in action: he truly was the most talented sales person I had ever met in my life with a passion that few people could ever match. I believed in him, in his business; and I trusted his plan would actually work.

When I returned and completed a trip report for my client, I recommended we accept the payment plan from the customer and continue to ship orders. My client's CFO was hesitant but agreed with my assessment. He had never been comfortable with the risk from afar but now was accepting of the risk with what I had found out: that the client would be at a cash break-even within 60 days and odds were strong that he would be completely current shortly thereafter. True to his word, the customer paid his account current, we kept the open dialogue with his lender and CFO, and we continued to make twice-yearly visits to discuss and assess progress.

The client who had struggled with his past for so long was finally able to overcome his difficulties. He settled the lawsuits, kept his vendor accounts current, opened up a large operating line with his bank, tripled his sales and grew his business into a cash flow powerhouse. He became the largest customer of my client within three years of that first meeting with him.

Many years later, after we had stopped representing the manufacturing supplier, the strategic business owner called me to see how I was doing and to tell me I was the best credit manager he had ever worked with...and that he missed me. Turned out he had sold his business to a large public company for more than $100 million...more money than he could spend in his lifetime. He wanted me to know how often he thought of me and how he appreciated that I was there for him when he was turning his business and life around.

I was so proud to have been a small part in his success and honored that he even remembered a lowly credit manager who caused him so much grief years ago. This customer situation taught me to look beyond the numbers and the history of the business to truly understand the existing risk to create solutions that will benefit everyone.

Pam Krank

Pamela Krank is President and founder of The Credit Department, Inc., a commercial credit management solutions provider that helps businesses increase cash flow and reduce costs by providing sophisticated credit management services, processes and technologies. These services save her clients millions of dollars in interest and bad debt expenses each year. Krank started the company in 1993 after 13 award-winning years in the credit department of 3M. She has been a regular contributor to *CFO Magazine* and has been featured in numerous publications including *Treasury & Risk* magazine.

Tim Paulsen & Ken Young

Wadda' Mean You Don't Want A Discount?

By Ray Casola

What's the True Price?

Some years back, we were approached by a customer who was looking to purchase a 'larger than normal' order from us. Naturally enough the sales department had visions of plum fairies dancing in their head but we pressed for not only the normal documentation for a new credit application but also financial statements.

All were provided in due course and information was positive...*for the most part.*

One source indicated the company was sold a few months back. This prompted us to ask more questions and we discovered the firm had been sold to an 'interesting' gentleman whose history included being kidnapped, a number of arrests, in short, not a typical customer and far from a shining example of a good corporate citizen.

The other troubling indicator was that not only was the customer trying to place a larger than usual order – they were satisfied to pay the full list price; they were NOT looking for any discount.

We asked to be paid by COD and all orders were cancelled. A month later we learned they left all of their creditors in the cold for some twenty million or so dollars.

Ladder lesson learned:

If the deal is too good to be true – it is. Sometimes you should look a gift horse in the mouth.

Nobody is dishonest in just one aspect of their life. A crook is a crook.

Ray Casola

He has over twenty-five years' experience in the chemical & paper industries. He has served on the Board of Directors of the National Credit & Financial Executives Forum as well as the Raw Material Credit Group. Ray believes whole-heartedly in the value of ongoing training as well as the significant impact of mentoring his staff and other Credit

Tim Paulsen & Ken Young

Professionals.

A Trojan Horse?

By Christine Fisher CCP.

'Guarantee' from Sales and a Verbal Agreement May Not Be Worth Much when Push Comes to Shove.

Late in the day towards the end of the month of July, we received notice that there was a sizable quote (267K) we were working on for our customer in Virginia. Financially, they were not great however one of our leasing partners – was involved and pre-approved $126K of the opportunity (without reviewing financials). This partner stated that if any new entities were introduced to the deal they would be subject to their standard credit review process and it could not be assumed that any changes to the legal structure would be approved. In addition, we were able to get them approved for $141K from another lender again, without sharing financials.

What this means is that we would invoice

these lending partners and they would fund us once the customer had received all the products AND signed a delivery and acceptance document. From a credit perspective, we evaluate the lending partners as they are the one's paying us and obviously ensure all paperwork is in place. The customer provided us with a written email indicating they would sign the lease doc's within 7 days. Our vendor agreed that the order was cancellable within 30 days in the event something fell through. The order was entered two days later in the evening and released for $126K.

In summary - the customer was approved for $126K by one lender and $141K from another – the lease docs were not signed however the customer agreed to sign them and return in 7 days. We had a 30 day window to cancel with the vendor/return the product. Our VP Sales claimed the VP of Operations at our customer was a close personal friend and their office was across from one of our branch locations. We approved the deal.

We were then informed that an acquisition had occurred and our customer had merged with another entity. The financials were then required showing the two entities combined with their new capital structure to our lending partners in order to be re-approved under the new entity.

Our leasing Manager took on the responsibility to follow up with the client (through Sales) to secure financials, to ensure we could get the deal re-approved and also to create new documentation for signatures with the new legal name. This occurred every few days.

After 25 days, the more we learned about the deal, the more uncomfortable we all were with the transaction. Financials were finally received and provided to our lending partners who denied approval of the deal that we shipped. The customer was advised that the product would need to be returned however they refused and indicated we would need to sue them to get the product back. Our vendor obviously did not want the product back either and gave us an additional 15 day return extension to allow the customer additional time to try and get access to some cash/funding for the product.

Come late August, the Customer claimed they were trying to get the cash together to make the deal work and pay us directly. After an additional 2 weeks of back and forth, the customer finally provided our lending partners with enough evidence/financial information to convince them to approve/lease this deal for them. We finally received the approval mid September and were able to send the invoice out for payment.

In summary and conclusion - the customer did not advise us at the time of the order that the acquisition would occur prior to the doc's being signed and returned. Customer did not sign docs within 7 days as promised and was unresponsive to the Credit/leasing team. Customer was not forthcoming nor did they act responsibly.

Our VP Sales appeared to be unable to leverage his relationship to resolve the outstanding issues and in fact, distanced himself from the scenario that had gone bad.

We acted in good faith ....based on an email/customer's word.....

What did we learn (the hard way):

- Have Finance/Sr. VP speak to their finance folks in advance to get their commitment/buy in on the transaction rather than funnel through Sales team.

- Do not approve deals when documents have not been signed with end users that are new to us (where we saw their financials and knew it would be a challenge to get approval). An option would be to impose a penalty/restocking fee drafted by the legal team relating to meeting the time lines on lease execution.

- Make sure the i's are dotted and the t's crossed pertaining to documentation! Beware of the huge, hollow, wooden Trojan horse much like the ones made by the Greeks to enter Troy during the Trojan War. Things are not always as they appear.

Christine Fisher, CCP.

She is the Credit Manager at Softchoice, and has been a Credit Professional working on both sides of the border for over 25 years in a variety of industries including Construction, Food, IT, Manufacturing and Distribution.

Christine holds a CCP designation with the Credit Institute of Canada and served on the Board for 7 years with the Hamilton Chapter including President from 2000-2002. She continues to educate herself through a variety of Modules from the CIC and NACM CBF Courses. Christine has also been a member of the NACM for 20 years and continues to be involved in their annual conference.

Saturday Night Special – on a Friday Afternoon

By David Holloway

The REPO Man

I have been in "collections" since the tender age of 17 and started out with a TV rental company in Ft. Worth Texas but I have worked in 8 states and Canada. Texas and Texans think of themselves as a nation apart from the USA and believe me there is no greater pride shown than there is in "TEJAS" so even though the law says no one except law officials & military personnel may carry weapons concealed or otherwise doesn't stop 75% of the population in Texas from carrying hand guns. The results show in the murder rate for Houston or Dallas...very sad.

The TV/Furniture & Appliance *rent to own* business was a tough teacher for my first venture into the collections field. We were called 'Account Managers' and worked hard as well as long hours. A person comes into the store and you sell them on something in the showroom, you sign them up to a contract and set a date & time for delivery and then made the delivery – this way we knew where our stuff was (or at least where it went). The customer had a date each month/week or whatever to come in or drop in the slot their rent for that period of time. No rent would mean that we go out and forcibly remove the item or items from the property as agreed to in the contract. You are correct if you assume that was not the fun part of the job.

At the end of my third week, on a Friday, the manager told me of a woman who had not paid rent in two weeks for her TV and a set of bunk beds. He neglected to mention she was on the 3rd floor exterior walk up in an apartment section known locally as 'the projects'. This meant a lot of folks in tough financial situations, often disabled and living on social assistance.

Something else the manager neglected to mention was that for a lot of people in the projects, the third Friday of the month was pay day. For those of us lucky enough to have a steady job, pay day is always welcome, but not so much a cause for celebrations. This was not the case for many in the projects and that meant there was a lot of drinking and barbequing going on with little '*hibachi*' grills on the tiny walkways and lawns so it looked like a big old party.

I spoke to our customer and the woman frankly admitted that she did not have the funds to pay what was owed and not likely to do so in the foreseeable future. She understood I had to take it back. I loaded the TV and 90% of the bunk beds and was going down the stairs of the third story walk up for perhaps the sixth or seventh time when I heard behind me from an uncle, who was not quite as understanding.

"Hey repo man, WTF ya'll doing taking my nephews beds and TV and sh. .come here and bring it back or you's gonna be a hurtin now," half way through his little speech I look over my shoulder and there are 4 large men, drinking Miller high life out of glass bottles and the guy in front doing all the talking was emphasizing his argument by waving around a snub nose 32 revolver, they used to be called 'Saturday night specials' for all the close range killing they did & were popular with gamblers and drug dealers as are small and concealable. The fellow doing all the talking (the uncle) was smaller than the rest, but the 32 made him bigger.

By this time, when he was half way through his speech and I saw who I was dealing with and the gun I had a flight and a ½ head start so I ran with the mattress to my van threw it in and as I come around to the driver's side beer bottles start flying and he starts shooting – I jump in & try to get the keys out – lock my door and by then they are on my side of the van just beating on it till they started rocking it and were actually able to flip it on its side, all in about 90 seconds though it seemed a lot longer.

That is when I noticed I had blood running down my leg & into my shoe.

I'm trying to get up and get away from the windows and use the mattresses to hopefully stop any more bullets when I hear more gun shots but much louder than the 32, more like 357 so I was really praying at that point when the back door was opened and a policeman had a gun pointed at me telling me to get out of the van. Lucky for me there were several patrols of officers on a permanent basis walking the beat, beefed up on the third Friday of a month. Once he had the situation under control and the ambulance arrived I could finally breathe – all this in under 20 minutes – holy cow I was in shock.

On Monday, after a weekend in the hospital, I returned to the office, planning to quit my job. I discovered the 'neglectful' Manager had been terminated and I had a nice card and a check for five thousand dollars to *help see me through any difficulties.* I'm not sure the card did much to help but heck, 5k when you are 17 years old back in 1979 was like winning the freaking Lottery!

The other 'account manager' at the store told me about Remco TV Rental needing someone and I should really go there cause the owner was totally cool and the only reason he didn't go himself was because he was related to the owner. I took his advice and met the owner "Bubba". (Oxymoron in this case as he was not very big fellow)   But I tell you: he knew people, how to solve problems, read people &

situations and that job changed my life. His brother ended up being my BFF – after less than 18 months in training with "Bubba" I ended up managing 6 stores in the Houston area & was living just down the street from NASA in Seabrook where I fell in love with the Texas coast – Galveston & Seabrook especially. Where else could you pull over, wade out into the sea with your pole & catch a red fish or flounder in a few minutes and go home with supper in the cooler or the shrimp boats with ½ pound prawns for a buck a piece? That job prepared me for many other adventures in collection agencies and "boiler rooms" to owning my own agency for a few years until I got bored with that and started a building supply business out of Blaine Washington. There I met a lovely Canadian who became my wife. We started a family and moved to Kamloops BC.

Advice - it has ALWAYS BEEN MY RULE to NEVER, EVER, NEVER live in or near the community to which you serve – I am sure you can think of problematic issues with having someone serve you a meal in a restaurant that you may have just sent a demand notice to or had to repo a vehicle from them or a relative.

So I never live any closer than an hour from where I work – besides the drive enables me to close that mental door on my day at work and switch gears to being a husband, father, drug & alcohol counselor......oh yes but that is another story. Anyway I hope you enjoyed my little walk, or limp in this case, down memory lane.

Remember, you are a problem solver and can make the difference in someone's life at the same time if you take the time to listen and work with the majority of your clients. Our delinquency is a lot lower with this approach compared to my predecessor's percentages. So, do some good along with the job and always watch your six – this is another good reason for the drive – always watchful & vigilant keeps you safe – but that is yet another story. After 38 years in this line of work which was just supposed to be a backup job until I got a "real job" I have learned a few things: be kind, professional and do what you say you're going to do without hesitation or prejudice. Watch out for problem clients and keep an eye in that rear view mirror – it only takes one seriously disgruntled client to really spoil your day – and never take your work home with you. Picture a big steel door in an endless brick wall, put all your work through the door and close it and don't let yourself open it until you return to the job – no one wins when you take it personally & home with you – believe me –

David Holloway

Originally from the United States, David has lived and worked in Canada since he chased (until he was caught by) a young Canadian girl. His work history includes credit unions, collection agencies, television and furniture rental, and the government.

Of what some may call the 'important stuff' he has been a drug & alcohol counselor and caregiver for the Elizabeth Fry Society for the past 17 years: taking youth right out of jail into our home for a stint anywhere from 1 month to 10 months while undergoing counseling & education or skills training.

One More Step, One More Try!

By Lily Soliman

I'm not leavin'

Back in the 90's, there was a major electronic retailer in downtown Montreal that was going through financial stress; serious rough time.

I was new to the collection industry and new to the credit group forums but was quick to learn that this retailer's situation had recently become a hot topic that always came up in the credit group monthly discussions as they owed in excess of $100K to major suppliers, including the company I worked for.

We had their orders on hold and had always been in contact with our Regional Sales Manager to help us with the collection, though he seemed to have lost hope because of what he had heard already in the market.

In February of that same year, our company was hosting their annual 3-day dealer show in

Montreal. I was asked to attend the event to extend credit when needed in order to maximize the retailers' buying power. I was excited because our delinquent retailer was on the invite list!

It was no surprise to me that they didn't show up on the first day. Mid second day, I asked our Regional Sales Manager to check whether our prospect was coming to the show. He advised that they had confirmed meeting with him at the show by noon that same day. Two in the afternoon strolled along and they were still a no show. By then, I advised the Sales Manager that I was going to the store to meet with the owner myself.

I instantly saw a look of worry on his face when he told me that he cannot leave the show to accompany me there. I told him not to worry and advised that I would take a taxi. "Not a good idea", he replied "but if you insist, then go, but ask the taxi driver to wait for you to make sure he brings you back! OK? Good luck Lil'!"

Without understanding or grasping his worry, I jumped into a taxi at the main entrance of the hotel and gave the driver the address. He was quick to inform me it was only four blocks away on the other side of the road. I told him "I know, but I have trouble walking in this cold and I need to attend an important business meeting for about half an hour. I will pay for your wait time to bring me back to the hotel". The driver quoted me a price. I opened my purse and gave him half of his quote on the spot. He dropped me off at the door of the store and said he would make a couple of loops and be back to pick me up in half an hour.

As soon as I entered the store, I found 2 female retail sales associates and no one else. I thought: "Huh. Not a successful plan!" Although there were no customers in the store, they both pretended to be busy. A lady standing nearby to told me to wait a second and started to make a phone call. She mentioned the owner's name and was talking to him for few seconds about a delivery. At the end, she told him that she would go see him right after she finished with a customer (who happened to be me).

When she asked me how she could help, I advised her that I wanted to meet the owner.

She dialed a number and advised the other person on the phone of my name, my company and that I wanted to see the owner. There was a true ½ minute silence from her side. Then she hung up the phone and said that the owner was not in the store and did not come in today.

I replied: "Listen, Mr. (his name) is here and I guess he can see us through this camera" and I looked at the camera and waved. "So please call him again and let him know that I will not leave the store even if he doesn't show up for few days!" I said.

She was shocked but dialed the number again and was whispering to the other person on the line. She then hung up and said nothing more to me. Ten minutes later a big, big, very big man came to me and asked: "Do you still insist to meet Mr. (his name)?" I had to think fast; the man was really big, biker style, big moustache and had no trace of a smile on his face! I replied, "Certainly, I will be thrilled to finally meet with him".

I followed him in the store, but I was puzzled; where is his office? Then he pushed a button and a big mirror starts turning around and there we walked a passage to a dark staircase to lead somewhere. At this exact moment, I understood the comment of our Sales manager and the look on his face.

For an electronics store I expected to see some related inventory; camera boxes, small TVs, audio systems. NOPE! It was kind of dark and there were two big bird cages and each with a couple of parrots staring at me while I was walking behind the giant man. Then, there was a light at the end of the tunnel, I mean at the end of the dark room! The man I was following pointed at a room and he told me to go there. He literally disappeared and then it was just the four parrots and I starring at each other.

I made big noisy steps with my high heels and stopped at the door. Finally, I see the owner's face. I looked at him before entering the room and I said, "You're missing a great dealer show and an interesting sale. I had to come to bring it to you myself!" The guy stood up and came to greet me half way in the room. As soon as I sat down I handed him the new product brochures and the paperwork for the show offers. I spent a good 5 minutes talking about our new technology and why he needed to give it his attention. The man agreed with me and he said he would place his order and come see us the next day. He also added, "By the way, I already mailed you the $13.9K last week." He went on to prove to me that he did by opening his system and showing me that the cheque number was issued, and cleared all the balance owed. I had to come closer to his tiny monitor to read the screen while he went on to swear that the cheque was mailed. He added while opening his desk drawer that no cheques by the name of our company were still pending. In the drawer I saw many envelopes on top of each other but the surprise was the first envelope was for my company. I stretched my hand and grabbed it. And I told him that his secretary probably screwed up.

The phone rang. He picked up the phone as I opened the envelope, and here was our cheque with the full amount. Now I needed to come up with an exit strategy with this precious cheque in my hand!

To my surprise, he said: "Your ride is downstairs". I didn't know what he meant. He proceeded to lead me to the door, then the stairs. Finally, I am at the store again and guess who was waiting for me inside the store? It was the Taxi driver. Apparently when the 1/2 hr passed, he came to the store to let me know he is here. When he asked about me, they told him that they hadn't seen me. The driver went crazy and told them he dropped me here and he had been watching the door for the last ½ hr and didn't see me leave and threatened that he would call the police! True story!

We left and he drove me back to the hotel where I was greeted by the yelling –out of worry- sales manager that I was late and I made them worried. I calmly opened my purse and I handed him the cheque. He couldn't believe his eyes.

I was still worried about the store's financial distress and there was a possibility that the cheque could bounce. A week passed after the deposit, it seemed that everything went alright.

Exactly 17 days after my visit, the landlord shut the business down and all other suppliers lost their money.

One more thing I forgot to mention earlier is that my company insured the receivables and this account was insured. We continuously reported the arrears. When the list of creditors got published I received a call from our insurance company to advise us that our name was not on the list. So I confirmed to them that we collected the debt 17 days before the closure.

Now that the suspense is over, here are the takeaways:

For a small insured debt, did I really need to go through this adventure to get paid? Not all adventures are safe; I was completely lucky on this collection. What made the difference is that from that incident on, our insurance company started noticing our unique capabilities. We also added a few more wins on other high-risk portfolios that were noted by our insurance as well. A company's credit policy and the strength of its credit management team has a value not only in negotiating your insurance price but also in determining the required ongoing coverage.

When collecting from stressed customers, it is better to understand how they reached that stage and keep strong communication with your sales team. Engage your sales management to work with you on a safe exit strategy.

If you know that all creditors are not getting paid, don't give up too fast. There is always one more call or a visit that may get you closer to complete your collection.

Lily Soliman

Lily currently is the Director of Credit and Underwriting at Samsung Electronics Canada. Lily has held other credit & sales administration positions at Samsung Electronics, Sharp Electronics and Daewoo Corporation.

For the last 10 years, Lily has been selected by her industry peers and voted as the Chairperson of the Equifax Canada Major Electronic Credit Group. This group meets regularly to review and discuss industry trends, and hosts the major retailers' key finance & operation management as guest speakers. Lily is also a member of the National Credit & Financial Executives.

Lily speaks 3 languages; English, French and Arabic. She graduated from Helwan University

Tim Paulsen & Ken Young

in Egypt with a Bachelor of Commerce & Business Administration.

The Road Unplanned

By Phyllis Miller Saavedra

Did I Do Something Wrong?

While I am sometimes reluctant to share this story, it was a valuable learning experience from the early days of my career. I should warn you that while I learned a very valuable lesson, at the time it did not end well. Fairly fresh out of college, circumstances and a need for employment lead me to a small crystal figure manufacturer in the sleepy town of Santa Barbara, CA. I was hired as a credit analyst with no finance degree and only a year of consumer credit experience under my belt. Two short weeks after joining the company our Credit Manager was fired and I was promoted to manager. Our CFO told me that I was smart, had a college degree and could figure it out. My survival instincts kicked in and I got a mentor, went back to school to fill in the gaps in my accounting education and joined several trade networking groups. I was on my way.

Learning to Adapt

Those early days were tough. Many, if not most of our interactions were antagonistic. Customers were either on credit hold or not. A "good customer" was simply defined as someone who paid their bills on time. Credit checks were simple; a good Dun & Bradstreet report and positive trade and bank references meant you got a credit limit somewhere close to 10% of your working capital. Exceptions were not considered. While we took great pride in being known as the "sales prevention team" I somehow knew that there had to be a better way of working with my peers, management and customers. Instinctively I knew that my behavior had to change if our business was to grow and prosper. I needed a whole new attitude if I was going to stand out and be successful. Don't get me wrong, changes did not come over night and have evolved and honed my behaviors over a long career.

Where Did I Go Wrong

It was around this time that I was approached by a customer opening a small gift shop. He came to me asking for a small credit line and net 30 terms to get his business off the ground. At first I said no, but he was rather persuasive. I agreed to a small line and said we would monitor his account on a sale by sale basis. For about 9 months he paid like clockwork. He even sent me a letter (email was not the norm in those days) telling me how grateful he was and how I helped him launch his store. I patted myself on the back and felt marvelous about how I handled things. I thought to myself, "This is how a business should be run". It was not much more than a few months later that things began to deteriorate. His payments started slowing and my collector was telling me that he was not returning phone calls. Eventually we were completely unable to locate the owner and placed the account with a collection agency. The balance was ultimately written off to bad debt.

An Unhappy Ending and a Lesson Learned

Several more months went by and I received a letter. To date this may be saddest letter I have ever read or received. The letter was from my customer. It was written on hospital stationary. He explained to me that he had tried to commit suicide because he could not make a go of his business. He wished that people like me had not aided in helping him to get started. I was understandably horrified. Where had I gone wrong? Did I create this nightmare? I was very young and new to the business world and I chose not to answer his letter. Others provided me with solace and told me that I should move on and take this as a life lesson. He was after all still among the living and had a chance at a fresh start. At this point I could have thrown my hands up in the air and used these events to go back to my old ways of guilty until proven innocent. I am thankful to this day that I had great colleagues and mentors who pushed me to move on past this and continue my journey toward being a team player and a corporate leader.

I did not share this with you to tell you not to trust anyone. I tell my tale for just the opposite reason. I know today and every day since this happened that I did the right thing. Irrespective of the outcome (you will likely never experience anything as horrific as this incident), you need to work with your customers. You need to listen to their needs and help them to be strong business partners. If they grow, you grow. You need to understand your company's risk threshold and on occasion, test the limits. Be a partner to your customers and your fellow employees. I am happy to report that since that day oh so many years ago I have taken numerous business risks and have yet to be let down.

Phyllis Miller Saavedra

Phyllis is currently Director of Analytics Services at Emagia Corporation. She has been working in the field of credit and collections for more than 20 years. Over the years, Phyllis has held senior management roles in companies such as Cisco, Aspect, Novellus, SanDisk and Saba Software. Additionally she has extensive experience as a consultant in all areas of the order to cash lifecycle.

"You Have a License for That Monkey?"[2]

By Declan Flood FIACP, FCICM. (UK)

Don't Keep Feedin' It

Early in my credit career, while still young and inexperienced, I attended a sales training course. One of the exercises they got us to do was to write down the direction we wanted our career to go. Even though it was over thirty years ago, I remember writing "To be recognized as the number one credit professional in Ireland." I don't know if it was the clarity, the simplicity or just the fact that I wrote it down, but that simple sentence has shaped my career since then and depending on who you talk to, there are times when I think I have achieved that goal.

---

[2] Question asked by Peter Sellers as Chief Inspector Clouseau of a monkey grinder as a bank robbery is taking place in the background.

My methods were simple: I first completed a three year Diploma course with the Institute of Credit Control in Ireland and as soon as that was complete embarked on a one year management course in the Irish Management Institute. The thinking here was that with four years' credit experience, combined with two qualifications I was on track to land a credit management position.

As you know, sometimes things don't go fully according to plan! I complained so loudly about the constant problems in the warehouse and distribution area of the business that I was offered a position to manage seven warehouse staff, the distribution and stock control function in addition to my credit control responsibilities.

This was the most difficult role I had ever attempted, and there is a huge difference between learning management on a course and doing it in the real world, to be honest, things got a lot worse before they got better.

I found myself going in early in the morning and coming home increasingly later at night, then the odd Saturday and even Sunday.

Before long it was every Saturday and every other Sunday. The funny thing was that it didn't seem to make a difference and the workload kept coming in waves and I was struggling to keep up. Still my ambition and pride made sure I would never give up and kept going to get on top of the constant issues that kept coming up. As busy as I was, it was fairly obvious that not only were things not getting any better, they were getting worse!

I knew that something had to be done. (Not only was I under pressure at work, now I was under pressure at home as well, with two small children that I didn't see most days and increasing absences at weekends) Desperate times called for desperate measures so I called my management lecturer looking for some advice. She listened to my story and recommended that I read a book. "Read a book!" I said "Read a book? Did you not hear a word I said? I am working eighteen hours a day seven days a week and you want me to read a book!" I couldn't believe it! Where would I find the time?

I found the time the next Sunday morning, I sat down with a cup of tea and the book called

"The One Minute Manager meets the Monkey" and it saved my life!

The reason I am telling this story here is that I hope it will be of help to you, as you make the transition into management or even if you are overwhelmed with things to do. There are lots of stories in the book, the one that had the greatest impact on me was the scene where the hassled manager was on their way to a board meeting and met one of their staff in the corridor. The staff member greeted the manager and immediately said "Boss, we have a problem" The boss listened for a moment, learned enough to know that a serious situation had developed and as yet, not knowing enough to make a decision. Now, even later for the board meeting they were going to, backed away with words like "Leave it with me" and headed for the board room.

The board meeting was a blur to the manager, who was thinking and worried about the implications of the meeting in the corridor and then took additional action points from the board meeting and headed back to their office.

As soon as they sat down, there was a knock on

the door – the staff member asked "Boss, have you had a chance to do anything about what we spoke about earlier?" The boss apologized and said, "No, sorry, come in we'll do it now."

Does this sound familiar? Could you have been in this situation yourself? Would you know how to deal with it?

Let's change the picture: Could you imagine the meeting in the corridor – except, this time imagine the problem in the physical form of a 200lb monkey, hanging on the staff member's back. As the staff member struggled up the corridor with their monkey, they were indeed happy to see the manager!

With the words "Boss we have a problem" The monkey placed one hand on the bosses shoulder and the other hand on the staff member's shoulder waiting for what would transpire. With the words "Leave it with me" – can you see what happened? The monkey jumped on to the bosses back, and the staff member skipped back to their desk with nothing to do.

The boss then brought the 200lb monkey to the Board meeting and probably picked up a number of additional monkeys there and brought them all back to meet the thousands of monkeys that were all over the office in various states of health, some were very sick and others were dying from neglect.

Fact is that if you are a constant "monkey-picker-upper" you will soon be overwhelmed and not able to cope. Fact also is that most credit staff end up with monkeys from every other department.

Very soon I realized this was what I was doing wrong. As my staff members came to me with their monkeys I took them! I took them all, to the point where eighteen hours a day seven days a week weren't enough to do everything. So I learned how to manage monkeys – simple! As manager, all I have to do is to define the next step for my staff and allow them to keep the monkey! So, in the corridor, instead of saying "leave it with me" if the manager said "Can you write a single page outlining how the problem occurred and include two or three possible solutions?" That way the staff member leaves with the problem and the tools to deal with it. Then on returning from the board meeting, the manager would go to their office via the staff member's desk to enquire how they got on with it. Chances are, 9 out of 10 times the problem will be resolved at that stage.

The manager can then enjoy working in a monkey free environment.

For me, in case you are interested, as soon as I finished the book, I went to the office for the last Sunday ever. Took my big pile of papers and turned it into eight little piles, one for me and one each for the guys in the warehouse. First thing on Monday morning, I called each one of them in turn and returned their monkeys to them one by one. As soon as the exercise was complete, I was alone and took a walk to the warehouse; they were all too busy to talk to me. I remember the feeling of finally becoming a manager in the true sense of the word, a manager that would never again take monkeys away from my staff, but help them to deal with them by simply defining the next step.

Monkeys can be action points, emails, pieces of paper, appointments, tasks or problems. As soon as you recognize them and learn how to deal with them you can begin to focus on the most important things and begin to make a real contribution to your organization.

I hope by reading this story and implementing the lesson you will come to realize your potential as a great manager, I would love to hear your story of how you made this simple lesson work for you.

The lessons are:

1. Know what you want

2. Write down your goals

3. Be careful what you wish for, it just might happen!

4. See "monkeys" at all times

5. Delegate "monkeys" to the lowest possible level

6. Keep your workspace "monkey" free

7. Life is short, enjoy what you do.

Declan Flood FIACP., FCICM. (UK)

Declan Flood is The Credit Coach and a lifetime credit professional, author, speaker and trainer on all aspects of credit. He can be contacted at

Tim Paulsen & Ken Young

Declan@thecreditcoach.ie. Website: **www.icmt.ie** . To receive your weekly inspiration from The Credit Coach simply send an email with the word "EZine" and your first name in the subject to be added to the list.

"Who Owes Who?"

By Alana White

Just Give Me A Chance

Two years of college ... I decided it wasn't for me so I went to work for a local retail store. I moved in to a position of front office manager. My responsibilities included counting the cash drawer prior to opening, verifying invoices, and making sure all special orders were placed with the clothing vendors. I will never forget the day that I was talking to the Accounts Receivable Manager in the back office. She was making collection calls. I told her that I could not imagine having to do that all the time. She said to always remember . . . "they owe YOU money; you do not owe them money". That really stuck with me but I had no idea I would carry that into the next phase of my career. After five years of being passed over for any promotions, I realized that they didn't want me to move up because I was handling all of their paperwork and special orders. No commissions were paid to me; however, the salesman and manager were doing VERY WELL!

After talking with my parents and my boyfriend, I decided it was time to part ways with the company. The manager was furious with me. He told me that I would never make it in the real world and the "boy" I was dating would never amount to anything. I am proud to say that I did not let his comments drag me down. The next day I received a very nice personal note from the owner stating that he was very sorry that I chose to leave because I was a very valuable employee. It's funny how my replacement was put on an incentive plan!!

Ten weeks at another retail store and I was hired as a credit clerk for Martin Industries which manufactured Ashley Wood Heaters and Martin Gas Stoves. The credit manager had just been hired and she was given an opportunity to build a credit department which had not existed in the past. I had absolutely no credit experience but I did have typing skills and she felt I would be a good fit. My first day on the job, she gave me a stack of statements and told me to send past due letters. I looked up at her with a funny expression on my face and asked "how will I know if they are past due"? At that time, I am sure she was questioning her decision to hire me.

Once I got my feet wet, I started making collection calls. Again, I never dreamed I would ever do that! I remembered what Helen said to me that day in her office, "they owe YOU money; you do not owe them money". The accounts were 85% past due when the credit department was formed. Approximately 18 months later, we were 85% current. We offered special terms for our heaters so businesses could stock up early in the year and pay on October 10th. This was a huge risk but I learned about letters of credit, financial statements, floor planning, and so much more. Norma Russell Chism believed in me. For 10 years, she mentored me, trained me, pushed me, got me involved in NACM and CFDD, and made sure that she taught me as much as possible. She was my boss but she was my friend looking out for me.

And also the job training paid off for me. I was asked to come to an interview with another local manufacturing company. Norma encouraged me to interview even though the position required a college degree that I did not have. During the interview, I made it a point to tell them that I DID NOT have a degree BUT I assured them that I could be effective from day one. Evidently, they believed in me, too.

Through the years, I learned that a good credit manager must be a good listener, negotiator, and baby sitter. I was always told that you can collect more bees with honey so I have always tried to be nice to my customers – kill them with kindness! The "Southern Belle accent" can only take you so far . . . there comes a time when you have to bring out the big guns and stand firm to collect. A new challenge is just around the corner!

Many, many stories come to mind but my favorite was when a collection call was made to a customer in California. I was told "I can't talk to you right now because we are having an earthquake". At the time, I just didn't believe her. The next morning, the story was all over the news!

For the last twenty years, I have been a credit

manager for Service Partners. In 2013, I was promoted to National Credit Manager which is a shared position with one other person. I have Norma to thank for my initial training as a credit clerk. Also, I am so glad that I did not listen to the first manager I had. I would love to go back and say "look at me now – and by the way, that "boy" that would never amount to anything has been my husband for 33 years. We have a great life with two beautiful daughters and a precious grandson".

Alana White

She tells us that Florence, AL has been her home for her entire life. She began her career in 1980 when she was hired as a credit clerk. Over the years, she has had the opportunity to work as a credit manager at three companies before advancing to the position of National Credit Manager for Service Partners LLC, based out of Glen Allen, VA.

They area supplier of insulation and related products. Their parent company is TopBuild of Daytona Beach, FL. She has been married for 33 years and has two daughters and one precious grandson. Their entire family enjoys the outdoors, especially camping and hunting.

But, We've Always Done It This Way?

By Lorne Booth CCP Emeritus. (told to and written by Ken Young)

Why Credit Limits Can Be So…Limiting!

I recall after starting at a new opportunity, looking at the aged trail balance and seeing account balances substantially higher than the credit limit posted on the individual accounts. I knew from past experiences that auditors always trashed the department in their report upon viewing this. What I then did was to approach the previous Credit Manager to ask him about this. He responded by saying that the Finance/Credit department is only on the hook for the value of the limit posted and sales were responsible for the rest. Limits he believed were only a guideline and he was very glad to keep sales going and people from all areas of the firm happy with him.

This was a new approach to me in all my years of credit and the courses I had taken, so I immediately requested time with my boss the V.P. of Finance who was also new to the firm. Routinely he was one to only allow a few minutes of discussion on issues so I knew enough to ask for more time. He was kind enough to take me to lunch so we had plenty of time for an in depth discussion.

I made him aware of the previous thought process on credit limits and let him know that as it stands right now, I am only responsible for about 50% of the receivables. For sure he was very surprised and said that "with you now being the senior credit person and responsible for the accounts receivable portfolio, are you happy with that approach to credit granting? If not what are you planning on doing about it?"

My response was, "by formulating a reasonable policy and setting up meetings with all the functional areas, this change would affect." The sales team, shipping, inventory control and customer service were a few of the areas that I would meet with. Sure I knew that I wouldn't be the great guy the previous manager was, however I believed in what I was doing for the sake of the company. Shipping to customers that can't or won't pay for product and leaving deductions unresolved for an extended period of time cuts into profit margins severely. Controls on shipments by the credit team are a must.

What I learned from this and it seems like yesterday even though it was over thirty years ago, was:

1) When you are new to a firm, understand the lay of the land fully and recommend changes if necessary. Don't carry old accounts receivable balances very long or it will reflect on you.

2) Find ways to get people on side with you. If they don't know the company policy, make them aware of it by explaining it further and why it was written.

3) Keep others (like the sales team)informed

4) Reaching out and involving others in the process will pay dividends.

"Do not go where the path may lead, go instead where there is no path and leave a trail." – Ralph Waldo Emerson

Lorne Booth CCP Emeritus.

Lorne Booth has held senior positions in credit and treasury management for over thirty-five years. He also has held direct sales and operations responsibilities.

He served as President and Dean of the Credit Institute of Canada, the Chairman of the National Credit & Financial Executives Forum, taught the senior management course at the University of Toronto, and has been active on various credit boards.

Lorne has been and continues to be an encourager and a valued mentor to many and a proud supporter of continuing education for those in the credit profession.

A Youngster's Learning Curve

By Cliff Mearns

Research, Research, Research

Why did we choose credit as a profession? The truth probably is that we just fell into it.

As a very young man working for an electrical business, I saw a newspaper advertisement for an office junior with a company I had never heard of. It happened to be the largest consumer finance house in the country; and I got the job. Over the next few years, I was promoted through various departments until I ended up on the credit desk, at the age of 17, with two stenographers and a dearth of credit experience. I was one of those lucky kids who had a becoming personality that beckoned interest from virtually everyone including my debtor portfolio; causing my arrears to shrink to a record low without cause for very many property seizures. I was promoted by being transferred to a new office in the far north of the country in the capacity of credit manager. There really wasn't too much structure or company policy relating to the credit granting process then.

Unless you lived in the 1800's and experienced the Wild West, you would be unable to imagine this place, at the time. So remote from the rest of civilization, that it was the resort of choice for fleeing debtors and anyone else wishing to avoid some turmoil in their life. Caravan parks were constantly monitored for vehicles that had disappeared; along with the debtor.

It happened one day that I felt it necessary to visit a debtor's house on the outskirts of town to find out why payments had ceased. Our security was a motor vehicle.

The house where the debtor lived was built on stilts, raised some 3 feet from the ground with 4 steps leading up to the front door. I arrived at the house and immediately saw the vehicle in the drive-way – the frame was sitting on brick piers held up at each corner. I headed straight to the vehicle. Not a single part was recoverable – it was stripped. I walked to the front door and climbed the steps. Knocking on the door loudly I heard muffled sounds in response – ultimately the door swung open.

"Hello", I called out not really taking in what I was confronted with.

"Hi", a voice replied. I still couldn't see anyone until I looked down and there standing on bare ground was my debtor. I looked again into the house and gulped in disbelief.

The floor boards were missing, the interior walls were ripped out; the kitchen sink hung in midair as did the toilet bowl. The bath tub, hanging precariously, was filled with rubbish.

"What happened?" I asked lurching over the guy on the ground, his head only just visible over the door sill.

"It's the way I like it", he responded.

"Is that my car out in the driveway that you haven't paid for? Where is the engine?" I implored.

"I sold the engine to buy a stereo." He replied.

"And the rest of the car; where are the seats, the steering wheel, the wheels and everything else?"

"I sold the wheels to pay arrears I owed to ABC Finance; the seats I gave to a mate because he had nothing to sleep on."

A bit stunned I asked, "So what are you going to do about the arrears on my account for the motor vehicle?" His response was, "well maybe I could surrender it."

I returned to the office, sat down and broke into uncontrollable laughter that returns every time I think about it.

What did I learn from the experience?

It taught me and most definitely my boss, to take more time in assessing credit applications. Credit can be a difficult role and at times frustrating, but at the heart of all collection issues is the debtor's capacity to pay. Take the time to research who you are dealing with before shipping the product, or providing the service.

Cliff Mearns...

...is a Registered Debt Agreement Administrator in Australia and has operated his practice since 1999 assisting financially distressed consumers avoid the consequences of bankruptcy. As Chair of the Personal Insolvency Professionals Association he represented the organization on the Bankruptcy Consultative Forum, a body that reviews bankruptcy law in Australia and has been a strong voice in the area of practitioner education.

He is currently working with Bond University, as the education representative of PIPA, to establish a course in personal insolvency for the profession.

Was It Something I Said?

By Michelle Davy

What's in a Name?

Something maybe I shouldn't have done, or rather, used a little more finesse in handling: After an endless four weeks beyond the due date of calling the accounts payable clerk of a retail store, listening to her promises, logging follow up calls, my patience had dwindled. At the back of my mind was the ever constant presence of that little inner voice telling me; "I might get fired for not collecting this one account". It doesn't make sense right? One account worth no more than a couple of thousand dollars, in the grand scheme of things, I should have known better. But I didn't. So the pressure was on.

On the phone to the very nice woman in payables, and after she told me the cheque was on the corner of her boss' desk, very politely, I asked if I could speak to him. After a fairly long pause, the man answered. I explained that the account was past due and that I needed the cheque that "his girl in accounts payables" had told me was on his desk. He flew into a rage, yelled and screamed that we would never get paid and then hung up on me.

Well, his words were all I needed to throw this one into collection. Called our collection agency "Creditel" and told them to remove the white gloves and hit him hard. Step 2, I called the sales rep to tell him this guy was on permanent credit hold. During the call to the salesman, he informs me that the accounts payables "girl" and the owner were husband and wife. It would seem I had personally injured the owner by calling his wife "girl". Somehow it didn't register with me he would find this statement derogatory, but clearly he did.

It took over 6 months to receive a call back from the salesman who wanted to negotiate a peace treaty. The debtor finally accepted to pay the entire debt and the collection fees we had incurred. He remained Cash-COD-Prepaid for 3 years for his troubles when I finally gave him a chance and reopened the credit file. None of the other suppliers were having trouble getting paid.

Looking back, I realize that I could have used the "girl's" name in conversation which might have averted a situation that probably didn't need to happen. Albeit, the debtor did bear his share of the responsibility for his own actions and bad temper.

Michelle Davy

Founder and President of CreditAssur Inc. a duly licensed insurance brokerage firm in Québec and Ontario. Responsibilities include advising clients on Credit & Political Risk insurance for domestic or international solutions tailored to the client's needs. Michelle's background counts 12 years as Credit Manager in mercantile credit, 4 years as Credit Insurance Underwriter and 10 years as an Insurance representative. Part-time author of Credit Industry related articles, Consultant and Advisor, Michelle aspires to assist Credit professionals through seminars, courses and in-house presentations.

Don't Give Up on Me, Baby

By Peter Kotzer (told to and written by Ken Young)

It's an Art not a Science

A popular song from a few years back included the lyrics, "These times are hard, but don't give up on me baby" and it seemed to apply to a situation I faced as a credit manager in about the same era.

It seems as though it happened yesterday. It didn't, but with the story being so vivid in my mind it might as well have been.

We had a client who owed a 6 figure balance to us (for advertising at a newspaper) and after climbing to that exposure we were advised by the owner of severe financial distress. The money owed to us could have easily been lost if they went out of business.

Numerous others in the same industry were either going bankrupt, walking away from their business or letting the firm go down and purchasing the assets for a song and starting up again under another firm name.

It was critical and prudent to find a way to assist the owner to turn the situation around so we would realize on our indebtedness. We knew from the start that it would be a long and difficult process to see our recovery and the turnaround complete. We had meetings after meetings over time and what impressed us was the fact that the client not only had a personal game plan that appeared to be viable but also that he kept us fully informed every step of the way. Sure, it could be said that we were rolling the dice but we had confidence, trust, and a strong gut feel (from years of experience) and a newly formed comfort level with the owner.

The client whose business was one of the largest fitness/health clubs in the city had ten locations. He looked at his firm more of a financial entity than the club that it was. His thought process was that with his goal of 20,000 members in a major downtown city paying about twenty dollars a month for membership, translated to four hundred thousand dollars per month. This amount times twelve months equaled four million eight hundred thousand dollars per year of revenue with a substantial gross profit on those membership numbers.

His overall objective was to turn the firm around by building membership to this level then sell off the firm to one of the worldwide major competitors who would desire to get a foothold in the marketplace.

We had numerous conversations where his lack of expertise was discussed. For example, when we heard of a number of NSF's his firm received, we recommended a third party collection agency to him. Again, the trust factor and comfort level was built as the business relationship deepened. Our value to him was constant advertising (full page spreads a couple of times per week) in order to successfully build the business. Their value to us was continued advertising/revenue on cash (for the new add) plus a percentage extra to pay down the old debt. We even applied all volume rebates to the old debt in order to help the cause.

Two years later we were rewarded by supporting him as the account was paid in full. Our client was also rewarded as the firm was built into a prosperous entity despite the initial setback.

To me the value proposition here is that relationships are the key. These are absolutely critical. Also, it is so important to listen to the full story. Take time to understand the clients' predicament, analyze the business plan to see if it seems viable and determine as best you can if they are being open and honest. Credit granting continues to be an art over a science.

Peter Kotzer

Peter was in the credit field for over 40 years, beginning in the retail credit card side of credit and collections at Eaton's of Canada, where he held a multitude of different positions within their credit operation. After leaving Eaton's, he moved onto the commercial side of credit and collections with the Toronto Sun Newspaper. During his time with the Sun he was responsible for many 100's of millions of dollars annually, as well as acting unofficially as the corporate credit manager, where he helped setup and/or restructure their credit departments in Calgary, Edmonton and Ottawa, along with doing bi-annual bad debt reviews of the Sun Corporation.

City Boy Credit Manager

By Robert Lorenzo

Don't Be An Outsider

I was born and raised in New York City and have spent most of my professional career working in the Big Apple. After working a few years in the credit department of a Japanese trading company, I was asked to accompany a salesperson to visit his metal buildings customer in Gravette, Arkansas, as they were looking for a higher credit line. The Japanese trading company I work for prides itself on the latest and greatest technology. The company has equipped me with a laptop, a hotspot, an iPhone and an iPad, which I normally bring on all my business trips.

Prior to all my customer visits, my homework is to learn as much about the customer as I can. I would search the internet for any information or news articles on the company as well as any information on the people I would be meeting.

If I had the company financial statements beforehand, I would try to memorize key figures of the financial statements.

Since Tulsa, OK, is the nearest airport to the customer, we had to drive two hours to rural Gravette, AR. The customer's property was modest and the office of the owner looked like it was built in the 1970's. Normally when I meet customers, I take notes on my laptop or iPad. For this meeting, my recording device was just a piece of scrap paper and a pen.

The salesperson and myself both wore sports coats, dress shirt and slacks, while the owner, along with three other colleagues, wore flannel shirts, jeans and work boots. I was able to tell right away that the owner and his colleagues were leery of me especially after knowing I was from New York. I decided to make small talk before jumping into business and brought up a positive news article of their company that I found on the internet. They were surprised and impressed I knew about this news article.

During the meeting, we discussed the company's financials. The owner mentioned a sales figure from the previous year, but said he wasn't sure that was the exact figure. Having memorized key financial figures, I told the owner what the exact number was and he went to his files to confirm. He was impressed again that I knew this figure. The meeting went very well and I was able to obtain the important information I needed.

At the end of the meeting, the owner did admit to me that he thought I would be a "snobby, know-it-all New Yorker" when he first met me. But he was glad I was the total opposite. After the meeting we had lunch in town at a local restaurant, which was one of the best southern food meals I ever had in my life.

The lesson learned from this meeting is to be well prepared and know your customer as much as you can. In addition, it is important to "read" your customer during the meeting. Are they comfortable talking with me or are they being apprehensive. Lastly, don't be an outsider (in dress, technology and communication style) that you've lost the connection aspect that allows for trust to be established and ultimately disclosure of private information.

Robert Lorenzo

Robert Lorenzo is a Director in the credit control department of a Japanese trading company in New York City covering the steel and non-ferrous industry with customers in the US, Canada and Mexico. Prior to this, Robert was in the banking industry for almost 15 years working for several banks including US, Japanese, French and British banks and covering several industries including, automotive, homebuilding, consumer, retail and industrials. He earned his Masters of Business Administration in Finance from St. John's University.

Give the Money Back?

By Carole Stevens

Relationships

My Senior Manager, asked me to review the preference claim we had just received from the litigation trustee demanding a very large amount of funds exceeding $ 100,000.00. I was not familiar with this customer account that had filed bankruptcy as it was before my time, and had no experience with a US bankruptcy, or the statutory and policy framework for this claim. *"The preference laws are intended to further the bankruptcy policy of equality of treatment between creditors. Within the ninety (90) day preference period some creditors received payments, but many did not. By forcing the return of transfers made during the Preference Period, the assets of the bankruptcy estates are increased. The Trustee is required by law to collect all assets of the Debtor's bankruptcy estates, including the recovery of monies paid on account of existing debt within*

(90) days before filing of the bankruptcy petitions."

I researched the above (google) ☺ and it listed a couple of options to pursue. Because it is a public filing, you can request all the unsecured creditors, and it has been noted in many cases they can prepare a case together, share the expenses, and one lawyer will defend their case. Other option: take the small settlement offer that the litigation lawyer offered, if the preference claim was paid immediately.

After discussing with my Senior Management team, they said try option 1: contact the other creditors. I immediately requested the public filings of all of the creditors, and reached out to all of them.

A couple of the creditors, advised they were just going to pay the preference claim, and be on their way, others indicated they had their own in house lawyers that would address it for them.

One creditor returned my call, a beautiful lady and CFO of a very large reputable trucking company who said she did not understand the legalities of how her lawyer handles these cases, but said he has a loop hole and they always succeed in reducing the amount of the claim by around 75%. She indicated they used to just pay the full preference claim upon request, after two years from the time the debtor filed bankruptcy. They decided they would try this lawyer that was passed on to her.

Another creditor reached out, a Credit Manager from a very large reputable company, advising the same information, and the same lawyer that has helped them in the past. She as well, indicated they have learned from prior Chapter 11 bankruptcies to save all contracts, invoices, statement of account, and all pertinent information, as this never fails. In two years, you will have to send all of this information into the lawyers to defend your case.

After forwarding this information to my Senior Manager Team, with the information we had and the hands on experience from two reputable companies with Chapter 11 bankruptcies, we decided to work with this lawyer. The lawyer upon request, asked for all the invoices, contracts, application, and all other pertinent information. This lawyer managed to reduce our claim of $100,000 to **$ 0.00.** I know! And his fees for this was $3,000.00, it was an incredible win for us. And honestly if it was not for the those two colleagues, who had been in this position before, and had incurred losses for incredible amounts in the past and were willing to share this information, so we could all be successful in this situation, a win/win.

In my 20 years in Credit & Collections, our DNB reports and Equifax reports and financial statements allow us to make sound decisions, but ultimately the relationships we build with colleagues, customers, creditors, vendors, and trades, is our greatest tool as that information is not in a credit report, or in an instruction manual.

Carole Stevens

Carole Stevens is a credit professional with over 20 years' experience in commercial lending and collections. She is currently the Credit Manager at Bison Transport Inc., and has past experience in consumer finance, lumber, government, and construction industries. Her collaborative approach to management fosters continual learning and training, and perpetuates her philosophy of continuous improvement.

Angry Customers are The Best Customers

by Stephen Coyle CCE.

What Psychologists Tell Us

As a new collector I was usually afraid of angry customers. I would often transfer them to my boss or a senior collector to handle. But this causes people to view you as 'weak' or worse 'incompetent'. Eventually I decided that angry customers are part of my job and I'd better learn how to handle them.

After a few calls I became better. My mindset shifted from one of scared collector to one of a curious detective. I wondered what in the hell was making the customer so angry in the first place. Angry customers became challenges and helped me break out of the routine task of making normal collection calls. In fact, I looked forward to collection calls and even asked my colleagues to transfer their angry customers to me.

The reason I enjoy angry customers is because

angry customers care. And if they care, they usually pay. It was especially challenging to get customers who say at the beginning of the call, "And I'm not going to pay you a single dime' on the matter to pay me balance-in-full by the end of the call. It felt like magic turning initial 'refuse to pays' into approved credit card payments.

I'd much rather collect from angry, irrational customers who care over rational, contented customers who refuse to pay.

After a while my bosses could see that I could handle these customers well and wanted me to help the other collectors in our department. They wanted me to create a model for them to use.

I created the following:

I call it AUSE, but it's really any tool to calm angry customers. It is also a problem-solving tool. I discovered that by calming customers and solving their problems; I often collected the money. The process I followed is....:

First, I acknowledge their problem(s) by showing that I was listening to them. At this step the angry customer is in charge and you have to let them get over the anger. This step can take a long time. At this step I usually throw a few 'sorry' and other empathic statements to help them calm down. NEVER tell the customer to calm down. NEVER still ask for the money. If you want customers to calm down and pay you, you first have to focus on their needs, not yours. Once you help them (scratch their back), they will help you.

Second, I understand their problem(s). I understand both the facts about why they are angry and the feelings behind the anger. Usually I do this by repeating or paraphrasing customers' facts and feelings, then confirming it. For example,

"Mr. Jones, you are frustrated that you still haven't received your credit note for $40, even after speaking with two of our collectors here, and now you want to cut your service, is that right?"

I've found by repeating customers' facts & feelings and then confirming them, is a powerful one-two combination that calms most customers. I have never had a customer get angry that I repeated their problems. Once they are calm, I can then take control.

Third, I solve the problem. I use words like "I will" vs. "I try", or "We will". Other nice words when solving problems are "easy" and "I guarantee". I avoid the word 'problem' and instead use the words 'situation', 'concern', 'issue', etc. Your choice of words can help diffuse the situation. I use the word "OK" once I explain my solution in order to get the customers' agreement.

Lastly, AUSE consists of empathy. I put the 'E' throughout the whole process, but usually I will throw most of my empathy when customers are at their hottest at the Acknowledge stage. My key word is 'sorry'.

Once you have completed the AUSE process, most customers are surprised that you listened to them and took ownership of their problems. Many are also surprised that you actually expressed empathy because many collectors simply focus on money. Customers will feel obligated to help you.

Psychologists tell us that humans have an innate need to reciprocate when something is done for us. What do you say when someone holds the door open for you? Why do you say it? How do you feel after you receive a free sample of something at a store and then not buy the product from the promoter? I use the need to reciprocate on angry customers. Now that I took the time to listen, showed empathy, and solved problems; I expect them to feel obligated to listen to me and solve my money problem.

Does this always work? Does anything always work? Of course not, humans are much too complex, but I guarantee that if you listen to customers' problems, show a bit of empathy, repeat their problems, then come with some solutions; you will have better chances to get paid vs. not doing these.

Good luck.

Stephen Coyle CCE.

Steve Coyle is an American credit & collections consultant based in Malaysia. He's the author of 'Debt Collections: Stir-Fried or Deep-Fried?' He conducts training throughout Asia and beyond. He's the founder of www.servicewinners.com

My Eight Year-Old's Description of My Career Transforms My Life

By Mark Silverthorn, Attorney-At-Law

Speedbump and a Midlife Crisis

I spent twelve years working as a collection lawyer in the Greater Toronto Area. My clients included some of the largest collection agencies operating in Canada. I was a collection industry insider and I enjoyed a comfortable life.

One day I asked my eight year-old daughter what I did for a living. She replied "You send people letters telling them to pay their bills or you will put them in the garbage". This little girl's comment had a profound impact on me. I felt like I had been run over by a tractor trailer. Would her answer be my legacy? Was that the footprint I would leave on this earth?

I began to think about what I had learned over the past 12 years and how that information might be helpful to Canadians struggling with debt. It was at this point that I began thinking about writing a practical book geared to assisting Canadians experiencing problems with unsecured consumer debt.

I subsequently found a literary agent and signed a book deal with McClelland & Stewart, one of Canada's oldest and most prestigious publishers. I spent a considerable amount of time researching and writing The Wolf At The Door: What To Do When Collection Agencies Come Calling that was published in January of 2010.

After writing this book I represented a significant number of Canadians struggling with debt. In many cases I was able to negotiate favourable settlements on their behalf. More recently I have become an avid blogger on not only the credit and collection industry but also those firms holding themselves out as assisting consumers struggling with unsecured consumer debt. I also make myself available, for a modest fee, to provide telephone advice to Canadians experiencing debt problems.

One simple statement from my eight year-old daughter completely transformed not only my career but also my entire life.

Mark Silverthorn, Attorney-At-Law

Mark Silverthorn is a former collection lawyer who--over a 12-year period-worked for four of the ten largest collection agencies operating in Canada. He subsequently wrote a book titled *The Wolf At The Door: What To Do When Collection Agencies Come Calling* (2010), published by McClelland & Stewart.

Mark is routinely consulted by the media on the activities of bill collectors and consumer debt. He is also an avid blogger. Mark Silverthorn is the Founder of Comprehensive Debt Solutions Ltd., www.comprehensivedebtsolutions.ca, a firm assisting Canadian consumers struggling with consumer debt.

Credit, Sales and Peter Drucker

By Andriy Sichka

The Best Salesman the Sales Manager Never Had

The topic of proper cooperation between sales and credit teams nowadays is extremely popular. There are a lot of authors who provide their recipe on how to sort out a conflict between the two. Some companies believe that tension between sales and credit is the 'natural conflict' which helps a company to progress. Perhaps there is some truth in this, as long as their management is happy, who minds?

Let me share a story. In the very beginning of my career, I was collecting outstanding loans working in the bank's security service. Belonging to such a reputable department meant that the general objective of the whole team was 'protection', so I was really doing my best.

A few years later I joined a production company as a credit controller. Every single thing I was doing at that time was dedicated to the protection of an asset entrusted to me by the company – the accounts receivable. Customers who do not respect payment terms and sales people who always try to abuse credit limits were my opponents to fight with. Trust me, I was dedicated and brave. That was really hard work, but I was enjoying it as I thought I was doing the right thing and a useful job for our company.

Obviously I was very proud of my protector's role, till the moment, when my CFO asked me:

«How much profit does a company get from the goods laying in the warehouse?»

I did not give him an answer, but that was the magical question and a turning point in my professional life! Without any other single word I came back to the obvious basic idea - credit exists to support sales. Business cannot make any money without selling its products to customers. Since that moment the number of my 'enemies' significantly reduced, as I started to cooperate with them.

Deeper thought about the basics of credit has led me to another axiom:

«Credit is an extremely powerful tool of sales, it cannot sell itself»

It is pretty simple - customers buy a product which satisfies their needs. Credit, facilitates a sale of a product by giving an ability to use the product without immediate payment, but powerless to persuade a customer who does not want it. Understanding of this does not change the basic principle of credit, where «a sale is not completed until it is actually paid for», but paired with another, saying «to expect a payment it is necessary to sell first». Both principles, by the way, are pretty clear to those, who have tried to run their own business.

All the above has persuaded me to build and maintain deep cooperation with my sales colleagues and customers. The closer I was getting to them, the better solutions I was able to find and the better was the performance of my portfolio. There were less and less overdue accounts and bad debts were trending towards zero. Equally important, my contribution became visible to higher management and not just finance. The Sales Director used to ask me to come and talk each time before making a decision concerning credit. It was at that time I understood what real recognition means - appreciation of what you do by those who use it.

Credit Management includes many tasks. Support of sales is very important, but for sure is not the one and only task. The function has many stakeholders and all of them have their own needs. Treasury needs precise cash forecasts. Accounting expects quality of records and provisions. Logistics want sales orders to be quickly considered and released. The Finance Director wants to see the lowest possible percentage overdue and actually would prefer zero. On top of all of that we should never forget about our customers. To succeed in the role, a Credit Manager should find a way to meet all the expectations.

Several years ago in developing a mission statement for our department, we tried to apply the process outlined in the «The Five Most Important Questions You Will Ever Ask About Your Organization» by P. Drucker. The second question was «who is your customer?», though obvious at first sight, it was actually the trickiest. The book suggests defining one primary customer and several secondary ones. Nearly everything is clear, but which relationship line is the most important for credit and for the business as whole? Finally, on one of our brainstorming sessions we looked at the problem at the new angle - for our stakeholders our service is most important, or who do we impact most dramatically? The answer came naturally as 90% of our sales are made on credit and 80% of our conversation time was spent with them also. If there was not provided an adequate credit facility then the sale was lost. The primary customer of the credit team services is sales.

Reading advice from leading credit industry practitioners I found one similarity - they all claim cooperation with sales as the key success factor of their career. Philip King, Chief

Executive of The Chartered Institute of Credit Management, speaking about his career, said that the greatest recognition of his job was reflected in the Sales Director's exit note: «The best salesman I never had». The view on the importance of credit management may vary from industry to industry. However, it will always be an important service facilitating sales of products. Quality of this service is the ultimate factor differentiating successful credit teams from others. In the end, credit succeeds by contributing into the success of others. Seems to be quite noble, isn't it?

Andriy Sichka:

An international credit management professional with many years of successful business experience. Managing partner in A. Sichka Consulting (creditengineering.com) and Development Director of the Association of Credit for Central and Eastern Europe (www.creditcee.eu). Successfully accomplished training and consulting projects in companies like JT International, Electrolux and Golder Electronics.

Scam Prevention

By Bob Simon

Who Are We Talking To?

Before I tell you about the scam that almost took us to the cleaners, allow me to give a bit of background. Our company has operated for 30 years and our credit practices were a significant part of our good health. These practices, even precepts, were not drawn from any one template nor were they static practices as from a single text. Rather they were the culmination, the evolution even, from talented and sharing professionals whose craft were, each, honed.

For our company, these included great souls including but not limited to: Jack Hatfield, Trident Seafoods; Mark Adams, Peter Pan Seafoods; Vickey Roe, Ocean Beauty Seafoods. All three were, in addition to accomplished credit professionals, pioneers in assembling the best of the best credit professionals, across the seafood industry in North America, by way of building a platform by which credit managers young and / or seasoned could communicate about 'historic trade experience' in real time.

So much credit information that is gathered reflects bank and trade 'data' that is aged. This can be good and it can be misleading. Certainly it is of benefit to "see" into the past by months or years how a company has managed their banking relationship or their trade payables. Nevertheless unless you have direct communication with credit professionals you cannot benefit from "real time" / current events.

Professionals like those mentioned above realized this and built a platform for credit managers to become acquainted so that the most current information could be shared. Not information, mind you about their own credit decisions! That was not the intent. Rather the most current trade experiences available - -for a credit manager to include in his/ her/ their credit decision making. Real time trade information, the privilege of becoming acquainted with credit professionals in your industry and appreciation for those who will share their [vast] experiences (including but not limited to a company's credit history] - - these are the tools each credit manager should develop and continue to school themselves by.

Not only did these professors build a platform of communication for those less seasoned but they also underscored the value in making sure you know who you are dealing with and to investigate it fully. One example is as follows.

In investigating the credit worthiness of a potential customer who submitted bank and trade references, we were one of several companies that experienced falsified bank and trade references. It seems, to this day, remarkable the devious creativity of some but let this, our experience, provide all due encouragement that investigators (credit professionals) must be certain with whom they are inquiring and receiving an historic credit reference from which to make a credit decision.

Here is the scam that occurred: A company (or more appropriate, a criminal) colludes to set up a false bank and/ or a false trade reference (or more than one) that provides the illusion of being credible. The company seeking credit may even be of a company name well known but the perpetrator might be misrepresenting themselves and not even associated! In due course the company seeking credit submits trade information (a bank, a trade) of reputable name but with false telephone, fax and/or email contact information. Upon investigating bank and trade references, thinking that one is corresponding with "the" bank or "the" trade reference, it is quite possible to, in fact, be in communication with a shill and the historic information and experience they report on is wholly fabricated. In this day and age, it is not only possible but easy to purchase a telephone number as well as a fax [telephone] number in the area code of choice and even to identify a 7 digit telephone number close to that which is or would seem accurate. Email addresses are even easier to obtain as we have all been recipients of outlandish email scam allegedly from banks and other businesses brandishing trademark art that is identical or near identical.

We keep our own data base, as best possible, of bank and trade information telephone numbers and contacts. We actively look up telephone numbers and use a 3rd party [Who's Who] data to assure ourselves that the bank and the trade reference(s), with whom we are obtaining information, are with the highest degree of certainty, from the business that has the name. Above all, it is also relevant, we have come to believe, to use that "sixth" sense a credit investigator needs to hone. If it seems too good to be true, reach out further to discuss the information obtained. We have called back, on another day, to re-request the bank/ trade information and also, frankly, to see what professionalism we experience in the second inquiry even a day or so later. At one point, another company (with whom we share trade experiences) explained to our company, they have made a telephone call in the afterhours simply to see if a person answers or what recorded message they experience.

Making a credit decision on a new company, we have come to believe, is different from investigating a customer/ company with whom we have history and our own experience. The latter, for whom we are updating credit, which we do once to twice a year, or in consideration of an increase in the unsecured credit level, is different we believe from assessing a company with whom we, ourselves, have not done business. Along this thinking, making a credit decision on a new company should

allow for additional time. Sales needs to respect that as excited as they may be to write business, the risk of fraud requires time to assure that the new company being sold to is credible in more than name alone whom they present themselves to be. The lesson I learned was to make sure you know for sure who you are dealing with. Take the time to investigate, ask the necessary questions, obtain various contact names and addresses and verify.

For our company it was these professionals, the professors, if you will, to whom we attribute our 30 years of good business health. Bob Simon

Bob Simon has been with NOVA Fisheries, Inc., in Seattle, since the company was founded in 1986. NOVA is a seafood processor, finance and engineering firm with production and sales in North America, import and export trade and off shore investments in wild-caught

Tim Paulsen & Ken Young

and aquaculture fisheries.

Finding a Creative Payment Route for the Debtor Can Be Key to a Claim's Resolution

By Steven Gan CPA., CCE.

Socially Responsible and Contributing to Society

Having lived in Japan for 15 years and operated my own debt collection agency in Tokyo for 12 years, I'm often asked about the differences between collections in Japan and the US. With all of my years of collection experience in Japan, I discovered a few important cultural perspectives as to how the Japanese perceive owing money.

Most Japanese are embarrassed about not having the ability to pay their debts. They want to pay, they have the volition to pay, but in most cases they may not have the ability to pay.

There were cases when Japanese debtors who

had every intention of paying their debt obligations, couldn't because they were unemployed with no source of income. When I ran into this kind of situation I would often ask if they were actively looking for employment. In most instances they were, but after Japan's economic bubble burst in 1991 and the economy remained stagnant throughout the rest of the '90's, many people, particularly those in their fifties and sixties, could no longer find work. They were either deemed too old or too expensive to hire.

In trying to understand an unemployed debtor's level of desire to work, some of the questions I asked included:

- How many resumes are you sending out each day?

- Do you call any companies directly to see if they might be hiring?

- How well are you leveraging your networks to try and get introduced?

- Are you available to work in any field including jobs that require a lot of manual labor?

For me, if the debtor was willing to do any kind of job then it was possible I might be able to help them gain employment.

I'm not sure how many debtors we helped through this kind of approach, but it must have been a few dozen. As you can imagine, when a fifty-five year old man who has been out of work for a few years finally gets the chance to start working again, he has a renewed sense of hope for his life, the well being of his family, and the future.

I'll never forget the time when one gentleman, Mr. Tachibana, showed up at my office with his three kids who were ten, eight, and five years old. Mr. Tachibana had fallen on hard times. He had lost his job, his home and was living in his car with his three kids. Tragically, his wife had also passed away a few years earlier and his youngest son had a serious case of asthma. Plain and simple, he was down on his luck. Finding a job where he was able to take care of his kids and work at the same time was challenging.

Mr. Tachibana had an unpaid mobile phone bill of about 220,000 yen (about $2,000) and through one of his relatives I was able to get in touch with him. I appreciated him coming in and explaining his hardships. I asked if he was actively seeking employment and he responded with a resounding "yes." He then looked at me as though I was the messiah who was going to lift him out of his economic and emotional black hole.

When I told him about our Debtor Employment Assistance Program, he was excited and told me he would do any job as long as it either paid enough for someone to watch his kids, or have his kids in the same location while he worked.

I also mentioned I knew of a small trucking company that could use his help delivering small packages in his car throughout Tokyo. Again, his eyes lit up with tremendous hope and after a few phone calls I sent him on his way to the trucking company where he was immediately put to use making deliveries.

About two weeks after Mr. Tachibana started working at his new job, I received a payment of 10,000 yen ($100) from his employer that went towards his mobile phone bill, knowing full well that at that rate it would take almost two years to repay the debt. Yes, it was a long time to pay off a relatively small amount of money, but in the end it was better than nothing.

Six months into the job, Mr. Tachibana was hired by the company to work full time, and after two years he was promoted to vice president. At each promotion, the amount to pay off the original debt also increased and it was settled within a year.

Every time we assisted an unemployed debtor in finding a job, we not only brought that individual back from the brink of economic and moral despair, but also helped them to transition back into being a constructive, productive, and contributing member of society. It was times like these when I was proud to think of my debt collection agency as being a "socially responsible and contributing" member to Japan's well being.

Steven Gan CPA., CCE.

Steven Gan was the founder and president of

Advance & Associates Co., Ltd. in Tokyo from 1992 – 2004. Advance & Associates was the first company to create and implement the before and after sales total credit risk management product line system in Japan.

Through numerous articles, publications, presentations, and television appearances, Steve greatly deepened the awareness and understanding of the importance of sound credit risk management throughout Japan.

Steve recently wrote the book, "Making It & Breaking It in Japan - My True Story of Songs, Sins, and Solitary," which has become a best seller in the areas of Japanese Culture, Business in Japan, and Japanese Criminal Justice. This story is a revised excerpt from the book. Promotional video link can be found at: https://www.youtube.com/watch?v=Zw0l3qPjsCQ

Mr. Gan is also a Certified Public Accountant, Certified Credit Executive, and a Licensed Insurance Provider.

You Wouldn't Believe the Dividends

By Ken Young CCP., CCP. Emeritus.

A Unique Personal Signature

I remember it vividly because it was my very first full-time summer job. My eyes were wide open to see, hear and learn what was going on in the real working world. The company was a large department store and the office I was in was the consumer credit office. There must have been at least a couple hundred people working in that department. What I saw stuck with me forever.

My boss, who I thought was about five years older than I was, seemed to me to be on the young side not only in age but also in attitude compared to most other managers at the firm. The section of the department he managed had about 40 people, most of whom were middle age women.

Every morning employees would start their work day around 8 or 8:30, so we were all hard at work when our boss arrived at 9 am. What I saw happen daily was a great lesson on how to build morale. Every morning when this manager arrived, he would hang up his coat in his office, and then proceed to walk around his entire department, saying good morning to everyone. Each employee was greeted by name (or by a friendly nickname) and often given a word of encouragement.

Employees couldn't wait to have that Manager appear and "give them the time of day" by referring to them by name and saying a few words to acknowledge their worth. It was a nice way for the manager to let them know they were important. People who had their heads buried in work would look up when he came by with big smiles on their faces.

To me, it seemed like this simple gesture on the Manager's part made their day. It was the only time I would see some of them smile during the day. It literally lit up their faces. I knew he was like a hero to them and if he ever asked them do anything, you can be sure that he wouldn't have to ask twice. They would get back to him with an answer and be glad that he came to them to ask for assistance. I don't think he intended for his daily round to motivate staff or build their self-esteem, but this was the result.

It was pretty powerful stuff for a young guy to see in an office environment – firsthand – the way this manager treated people, built rapport, and demonstrated caring. Although it was just his way of starting the morning – as for others it might be checking their flood of emails – it made a huge impact on the department's morale and results. His unique, personal signature of interaction with staff probably only took him an additional ten minutes per morning, but the payoffs were very evident.

Things don't always go well, but it's a lot easier to cross the river when you've taken the time and effort to build a bridge. *How to Win Friends and Influence People* is a great book, but to see an aspect of it in action at my first experience in an office environment was something I'll never forget.

In leadership, if you establish yourself with a reputation as a supportive team player and unite the team with enthusiasm for a common vision, you are well under way to achieve success and reap immeasurable dividends.

"Kindness is a language which the deaf can hear and the blind can see." ~ Mark Twain

Ken Young, CCP, CCP. Emeritus.

Ken Young has been a credit management professional for over twenty-five years and has global experience in a broad range of industries including the food (aquaculture & beverage), chemical, manufacture, and transportation sectors.

Most recently he was the Credit & Collection Manager at PepsiCo Beverages Canada.

Ken was a founding member and advisor of NACM Canada (National Association of Credit Management). He has served on numerous boards, including the Credit Institute of Canada, the National Credit & Financial Executives' Forum, the Raw Material Credit Group and the International Center for Professional Collectors.

He has been awarded the highly esteemed CCP Emeritus award from the Credit Institute of Canada for distinguished and meritorious service for the advancement of credit education and the credit profession.

Consulting projects and keynote speaking with ICPC (International Centre for Professional Collections) include Brunei and Jamaica. He can be contacted at young.ken@hotmail.com or www.trpaulsen.com/credit

Balancing Ego and Humility

By Bill Lindala

Doing the Right Thing, the Right Way

In the collection business, it is almost impossible to find someone who isn't a bit of an egotist. We disguise that with words like confidence and high self-esteem, but we are all at least a little egotistical.

I worked for a company a handful of years ago and my title was, Supervisor of Training and Quality Assurance. In simplest terms, I trained new and existing employees and I was also responsible for making sure they stayed compliant on the phone.

In my role, I often took escalated calls and in some cases just took the call because the representative didn't feel comfortable handling the situation, especially if it was a call from an attorney. In one such call, I talked with a paralegal on an account for one of their clients that was filing bankruptcy. I don't recall the exact conversation, but the fact was that she was trying to tell me that we had done something wrong, even though we hadn't. I proceeded to make it clear to her that she was incorrect and had my feet firmly planted with my stance. My ego was strong in that conversation.

Little did I know, as soon as our call concluded, she called back immediately and got my manager on the phone. She explained the situation and how I handled myself and basically told my manager that we are lucky that they just don't file suit against us and work out the details later. He talked with her, smoothed everything over and practiced true humility.

When he was done, he sent an email to me, and copied the director of our department and Human Resources. He explained what I did, and what he prevented and said that he should never have to take a call like that about me, since it is my job to make sure that things like that don't happen in general. Then he typed these words that I will never forget:

"You are no different than anyone else."

I was thankful to be taught a lesson in humility and not at the cost of the company being sued or losing my job. I have since learned to balance the ego that is inside of me, while still practicing humility.

Bill Lindala

Bill Lindala has been a part of the collection industry since 1990 and has been involved in all aspects of the agency business. He has worked primarily in the third party collection arena in marketing, daily operations, compliance and training.

Through ACA International, he has served as a Certified Instructor, is a Professional Collection Specialist and achieved the designation of Trainer Specialist.

In addition, Bill has written several articles about the collection industry that have appeared in state and national publications, and he has also been asked to speak at various industry functions.

Learning to Build the Foundation

By Tracey Skipp MBA., CCP.

Don't Be Out of the Loop

It could be argued that none of us would be where we are today if it wasn't for the mentors who have given us guidance throughout our careers and passed on their knowledge and expertise. As experienced business people, we also have a duty to repay that mentorship and pay it forward to newcomers to our companies and industries.

Mentors are often found in our own companies, but for me, my most important mentors came from a trade group that I belonged to early in my career. It is unfortunate that not all companies believe in the value of these groups, as the relationships and the information gleaned from trade group membership gives us some of the most valuable tools that we can have when making credit decisions. Yes, there is usually a monetary cost to travel to meetings, but it is recouped many times over when it saves our companies from a bad debt (as it so often does).

My first high level position in my career was as Credit Manager for a steel mini mill. I knew enough about credit, finance and collections, but quickly learned that I needed to become familiar with the industry and the customers in order to be an effective Credit Manager for my company.

It was certainly a fascinating industry, and there were some interesting characters in it. Like the customer in the deep South who started preaching to me when I went to see his company financials in his office. To this day I'm not sure if it was a ploy to make sure I would wrap up the meeting quickly and get out of his office without asking too many questions about his business!

To help me be effective at my job, I joined a trade group consisting of other Credit

Managers of steel mini mills from across North America, and that group proved to be my most valuable resource throughout my time with the company. The group consisted of many knowledgeable, fun and friendly people, and they were happy to share their knowledge and expertise with me. Yes, we had some good times and laughter over dinner and various beverages, but we also had numerous serious discussions about our customers and our industry that not only saved my company hundreds of thousands of dollars in bad debts, but also helped me to be a more effective manager for my company.

There were only 2 other Canadian members of the group, and both of them had been in the steel industry for many years and were highly knowledgeable about the industry and the customers. Over the 10 years that I was in that industry, the three of us formed a bond, as we often travelled to the group meetings together and spent a lot of time together. I knew I could always call on either of them if I had an issue with a customer, or was unsure if a customer was having financial problems. We built a life-long trust and friendship that endures to this day. Although they have long since retired, we still get together for a chat about old times, the steel industry, the stock market and life in general.

The lesson I learned and would like to convey is that people who have been in your industry for years (like the people that were part of my trade group) have a wealth of knowledge and are generally very happy to share that information. Develop those business friendships and mutually share information. You will be glad you did.

Tracey Skipp, MBA, CCP.

Tracey has been in the credit profession for over 30 years working in a wide variety of industries including steel mills, tractor-trailer parts, software, and furniture manufacturing. She is currently the Corporate Credit Manager for Magnussen Home, a global furniture manufacturer selling to retailers around the world.

Tracey has an MBA from Wilfrid Laurier University and a CCP from the Credit Institute of Canada. She is currently 1st Vice President of the Credit Institute of Canada and is also on the Board of Directors for the National Credit &

Financial Executives Forum (NCFEF). She has formerly been chair person of the NACM National Steel Mill Credit Group, The Conestoga Chapter of the Credit Institute, and The National Credit & Financial Executives Forum

Tim Paulsen & Ken Young

Got a story to share?

Maybe you've been thinking, *"I've got a story as good as that"*, perhaps even, *"I've got a story better than that one."* It doesn't do any good to keep it to yourself.

We plan to publish a second edition of "The Mentorship" in November of 2017 as long as we have another fifteen or so submissions.

People want and need to hear your story of snakes and ladders in the credit and collection business. For the present, we are restricting to authors 55 years and up or with 25 years experience in the credit/collection business. (Quick test: If you know the machine in the image, you may qualify.)

The process is simple. Put your story together and send to one of us. As long as we have at least another fifteen stories to share – we will publish the next edition.

tim@trpaulsen.com

young.ken@hotmail.com

Made in the USA
Monee, IL
03 November 2020